OBAMA

THE ESSENTIAL GUIDE TO THE DEMOCRATIC NOMINEE

His character, his career and how he made history

Edited by NAFTALI BENDAVID

Triumph Books and colophon are registered trademarks of Random House, Inc. This book is available in quantity at special discounts for your group or organization. For further information, contact:

Triumph books

542 S. Dearborn Street, suite 750, Chicago, Illinois 60605

Phone 312-939-3339; Fax 312-663-3557

Printed in U.S.A.
ISBN: 978-1-60078-195-7

Cover and back photos by Zbigniew Bzdak, Chicago Tribune
Pages 6-7
Sen. Barack Obama and chief political strategist David Axelrod travel to a campaign event in Coralville, Iowa, in January 2008.
Pages 8-9
Several thousand students gathered at George Mason University in Fairfax, Va., to hear Obama speak in February 2007.
Pages 10-11
Obama attends a meeting in his office on Capitol Hill in November 2005.

"If we are willing to work for it, and fight for it, and believe in it,

then I am absolutely certain that generations from now, we will be able

to look back and tell our children that this was the moment when we began

to provide care for the sick and good jobs to the jobless; this was the moment

when the rise of the oceans began to slow and our planet began to heal;

this was the moment when we ended a war and secured our nation

and restored our image as the last, best hope on Earth.

This was the moment – this was the time – when we came together

to remake this great nation so that it may always reflect our

very best selves, and our highest ideals."

Barack Obama on June 3, 2008, in St. Paul,
upon claiming the Democratic nomination for president

Contents

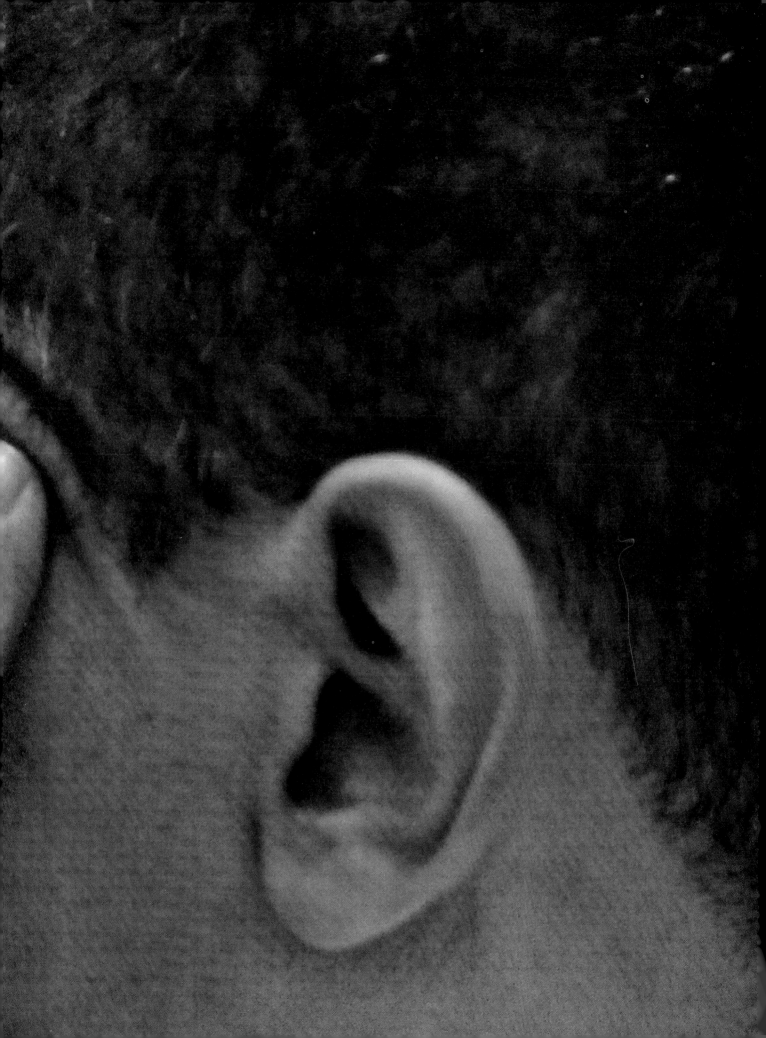

This book is based on the reporting of

Kim Barker, Mike Dorning, Ray Gibson, David Jackson,
Bruce Japsen, Tim Jones, Ray Long, John McCormick,
Flynn McRoberts, Christi Parsons, Rick Pearson,
Maurice Possley, Kirsten Scharnberg, Bob Secter
and Mike Tackett

Introduction: The phenomenon

A FEW DAYS BEFORE the 2008 Iowa caucuses, pollster J. Ann Selzer scanned the results from her firm's latest survey and found the numbers striking. Unlike virtually every other poll, this one, conducted on behalf of The Des Moines Register, showed Barack Obama comfortably winning the Iowa caucuses. Selzer's findings suggested something new was afoot: Independents and first-time voters were passionately supporting Obama and would flood the caucuses to ensure his victory. Selzer had confidence in her methods, but still she was surprised at some of the findings. "Of course that raised an eyebrow," she said. "Of course it did."

Yet the prediction of a surge by the young senator from Illinois mirrored what Selzer was finding in her daily life in Iowa. "It was as if the Earth were beating. There was a palpable pulse of excitement here," she said. "People were paying attention that had not been paying attention before. Among the normal people in my village — at the hairstylist, the cleaners — there was a far more enthusiastic discussion of the things that were going on. A lot more intensity than in 2004, a lot more. You just had this sense that something important was going to happen."

Selzer is a friendly, curly-haired woman who sings in the Des Moines Choral Society. She's been a pollster for decades and is thought to have an almost mystical power to divine the sentiments in the notoriously complex Iowa caucuses. She was not prepared for the furious reaction to her poll. Many political experts simply did not believe that Obama, a relative novice, could knock off Hillary Clinton in Iowa; Clinton, a New York senator and former first lady, seemingly had had every advantage and had led the national polls for a year.

Few were more upset than Clinton's staffers, who recognized that the poll, commissioned by the state's most prominent newspaper, could influence voters to go with Obama at the last minute if they saw him as having

the momentum. Caustic Clinton strategist Mark Penn dashed off a harsh memo deriding Selzer's methods in pointed terms. Another top Clinton adviser, Ann Lewis, called the poll's results "out of whack." Aides to former Sen. John Edwards were similarly dismissive. "Is the poll accurate? There are good reasons to think it is NOT," said a memo from Edwards pollster Harrison Hickman. Even some in Obama's camp, gleeful as they were, privately questioned Selzer's work.

And it wasn't just the candidates who were skeptical. The Des Moines Register's own columnist, David Yepsen, the most influential voice in Iowa politics, seemed to distance himself from the findings the day they were released. "No polls are predictors," Yepsen wrote in a column accompanying the poll, stressing that any number of last-minute developments could still reshape the race.

Selzer was taken aback. After the Register published the poll on Jan. 1, 2008, she gave interviews to C-SPAN and CBS News, then returned to her office and a host of emotional voice mails about the poll's findings. "Here comes all the stuff—wow," she said. "This has turned out to be a big deal. At the time it was a very uncomfortable and difficult situation to be in."

The reaction reflected how hard it was for even seasoned analysts to see that the nation's political landscape was shifting in an entirely unforeseen direction. Barack Obama, with a Kenyan father and a foreign-sounding name, unknown outside Illinois just four years earlier, was about to catch fire. The poll was the first glimmer of a political phenomenon.

Its results were essentially on-target. Selzer had found that this was a different kind of race, that far more people would attend the caucuses than ever before. Over the next few days, Obama's Iowa crowds, already impressive, grew larger and more enthusiastic, and Obama himself visibly gained confidence as caucus day

On caucus night in Des Moines, Sen. Barack Obama arrives onstage with his wife, Michelle, and their children, Malia and Sasha, in January 2008.

approached. In Ames, about 1,000 people waited for Obama for more than an hour. In Sioux City, more than 500 people showed up to hear him at Irving Elementary School, forcing 200 into an overflow room. "It looks like we just might do this thing," Obama told them exuberantly. It was not entirely clear whether the audience members were there out of curiosity or could be counted on to vote for Obama, but the campaign was hopeful.

On Jan. 3 itself, as voters headed for the caucuses a little after 6 p.m., on some streets virtually every garage door could be seen opening all along the block. At Merrill Middle School in Des Moines, the building's lights blazed in the winter night; some caucusgoers had to park several blocks away, and they trudged over icy sidewalks,

gathering to talk in groups of four or six as they headed into the caucus. Just after 8:30 p.m. Central time, CNN called the caucuses for Obama. "Barack Obama, a young man in his mid-40s, has now won the Iowa caucuses," CNN's Wolf Blitzer said, as if he could hardly believe it. Bill Schneider, the network's political analyst, picked up on the night's theme, observing, "Barack Obama has won an overwhelmingly white state."

The victory was remarkable for many reasons. Obama had defeated Hillary Clinton, a celebrity powerhouse with a formidable political machine. He had beaten former Sen. Edwards, who had spent almost four years laying the groundwork for his Iowa run. And he had overcome an array of other politicians with impressive résumés: Sen. Joe Biden of Delaware, Sen. Chris Dodd of Connecticut, Gov. Bill Richardson of New Mexico. First-time voters had indeed flocked to the caucuses, and participation almost doubled from four years earlier, to 239,000. In dismissing Selzer's poll three days earlier, Edwards adviser Joe Trippi had told The New York Times, "You'd have to have 220,000 people voting for that poll to be right. If that's what's going on, there's no historic model for it."

Trippi was right, though not in the way he intended. There was no historic model for what had just happened. For one thing, the American public had never confronted the prospect of a non-white president. Now, in one night, that prospect had become real. A black presidential candidate had for the first time won large numbers of white votes when it counted.

Beyond race, Obama had won the first presidential contest of 2008 by shrewdly presenting himself as the embodiment of change—not just from the sour Bush years, but from a far longer era of ideological, political and racial division. Obama had risen from obscurity to prominence in 17 minutes, with an electrifying speech to the 2004 Democratic National Convention. Had he lost decisively in Iowa, his presidential run would have been over. Instead, it would now surge ahead. For three years he had been a phenomenon, a gifted politician, a dazzling flash across the political landscape. Now he was for real.

Not that his triumph was conclusive — far from it. Clinton proceeded to defeat Obama in the very next primary, in New Hampshire, setting off a battle in which the two traded punches, and victories, until the final day of primary voting five months later. Clinton was the first woman to make a credible run at the presidency, and like Obama she embodied the pent-up aspirations of millions. It was the special poignancy of the 2008 Democratic primaries that the first woman with a credible chance at the White House faced off against the first African-American. Obama prevailed in the end mostly because his campaign strategists turned out to be much smarter than Clinton's. Even after her concession speech at the end of the long primary season, some Clinton enthusiasts refused to accept the outcome, seeing Obama as an unqualified interloper who had cheated Clinton out of the nomination. Despite efforts to pull the Democratic Party together, PUMA groups sprang up, the acronym standing for "Party Unity My Ass."

Amid this bitterness, it was easy to overlook the magnitude of Obama's accomplishment in capturing the nomination. In the memory of many Americans, schools throughout the South had been segregated. Blacks could not share certain hotels, pools or restaurants with whites. African-Americans endured separate drinking fountains and restrooms.

Just 60 years before Obama's rise, Strom Thurmond had run for president on the explicitly segregationist Dixiecrat ticket, winning four states. In one speech Thurmond assured supporters, "I want to tell you, ladies and gentlemen, that there's not enough troops in the Army to force the Southern people to break down segregation and admit the nigger race into our theaters, into our swimming pools, into our homes and into our churches." In 1961, black and white Freedom Riders, testing their right to ride buses together, were beaten bloody with baseball bats, iron pipes and bicycle chains. In 1963, 45 years before Obama won the Alabama Democratic primary, the state's newly elected governor, George Wallace, declared, "I draw the line in the dust and toss the gauntlet before the feet of tyranny and I say, 'Segregation today, segregation tomorrow, segregation forever!'" Obama would fill arenas with enthusiastic white supporters, but barely four decades earlier, he would not have been able to drink at the same water fountain as those supporters in some parts of the country.

But beyond the killings and beatings of the civil rights movement, and despite the progress, quieter biases and unofficial segregation persist. The strength of ongoing racial prejudice is hard to gauge; in some ways Obama's candidacy will present a test of its endurance. Without a doubt, racial conditions have improved markedly in recent decades. Black income and education have risen. Two-thirds of white Americans say they have a black neighbor, while fewer than half did in 1984. On the diplomatic stage, Colin Powell and Condoleezza Rice have spent eight years between them as America's face to the world. The culture, too, is changing. In November 2001, the Fox network introduced its hit series "24," featuring an appealing black president named David Palmer. The actor who played him, Dennis Haysbert, thinks the role helped pave the way for Obama's rise. "If anything, my portrayal of David Palmer, I think, may have helped open the eyes of the American people," he has said.

Yet some churches, neighborhoods, schools and workplaces remain highly segregated. African-Americans trail in every significant social benefit, from health care to income to education. One expression of the distance still to be traveled is found in the United States Senate, Obama's own institution. If he wins the presidency, trading in the Capitol for the White House, the Senate will lose its only African-American member. That would leave a country whose population is about 13 percent black with no black senators. Similarly, the nation has only one elected black governor, Deval Patrick of Massachusetts. Simply put, whites rarely vote for

"It would not have been possible 40 years ago for this candidacy to be launched.
It would not have been possible 20 years ago for this candidacy to be viable."

Wade Henderson, Leadership Conference on Civil Rights

African-Americans in large numbers. About 40 members of the U.S. House of Representatives are black, but virtually all of them represent districts with large black populations.

This gives some sense of Obama's accomplishment. His candidacy at least raises the question of whether the country is changing in some deep way, whether for all our racial sins, we are ploddingly moving beyond a history that includes slavery, civil war, segregation and lynching. Certainly watching a black man take the stage as a presidential nominee is breathtaking for some viewers. "This campaign and his victory in the Democratic primary signify a turning point in American politics," said Wade Henderson, executive director of the Leadership Conference on Civil Rights. "It would not have been possible 40 years ago for this candidacy to be launched. It would not have been possible 20 years ago for this candidacy to be viable."

Obama's campaign is prompting many people, black and white, to rethink their assumptions about America. The uneasy secret of presidential campaigns is that, with a few exceptions, presidents can actually do very little to affect citizens' day-to-day lives. Candidates make sweeping promises, but in truth most Americans' lives do not change markedly based on who wins a given presidential election. The political system is simply too resistant to change. What presidents can do, however, is deeply affect how we feel about the sort of country we live in. Obama's candidacy is rewriting the way many Americans view their nation's character. Obama — like other politicians, if perhaps more eloquently—promises to move the country beyond its racial and cultural divisions. But he also argues that he personally embodies that change and suggests, though not explicitly of course, that simply by electing him the country would show itself to have reached a higher moral plane.

That message infuriates those who see it as a way to dismiss opponents and critics. But others find it not only persuasive but inspiring. If the Obama candidacy is unique because of his race, it's also unusual in the impassioned dedication of his followers, the sense that he leads a movement, not just a campaign. Obama's candidacy has prompted millions of Americans to register to vote. It has sparked young people and new

voters not only to support his campaign but to throw themselves into organizing and working for it. The Obama phenomenon recalls a less jaded time before Watergate, when Eugene McCarthy could evoke true belief and Robert Kennedy could inspire an almost religious devotion.

Much of this has to do with Obama's soaring oratory and rapturous crowds. In the age of television and the Internet — those dismal filters of passion — it had been long since a candidate was known for the mesmerizing power of his speeches. An address at Iowa's Jefferson-Jackson dinner in November 2007 gave Obama critical momentum in that state. A speech in Philadelphia on race was praised by some as the best in a generation. After an unexpected loss in New Hampshire, Obama mused on the nation's historic determination to overcome its difficulties. "When we have faced down impossible odds, when we've been told we're not ready or that we shouldn't try or that we can't, generations of Americans have responded with a simple creed that sums up the spirit of a people: Yes, we can," Obama said. "It was a creed written into the founding documents that declared the destiny of a nation — yes, we can. It was whispered by slaves and abolitionists as they blazed a trail toward freedom through the darkest of nights — yes, we can." The musician will.i.am, leader of the Black Eyed Peas, set the speech to a melody in a widely watched video.

As for Obama's audiences, they have no recent match in size and enthusiasm. In this way, if no other, this is a new brand of politics. In February 2008, about 17,000 people packed Dallas' Reunion Arena for a glimpse of the candidate, applauding not only when Obama spoke, but even when he took a quick break to blow his nose. In April in Philadelphia, 35,000 people crammed into Independence Mall to hear Obama speak. In May, Obama more than doubled that, drawing 75,000 people in Portland, Ore., under the hot sun, thought to be the largest political rally in the state's history. These crowds do not always signify victory — Obama decisively lost the Pennsylvania primary, for example — but they reflect a striking engagement at a time when voters have often been content to watch campaigns unfold on television.

And yet, despite the poetry of his words and the idealistic aura surrounding his campaign, Obama has harder, more practical edges. He remains a politician, one who has not hesitated to play the game with a full appreciation for the necessary compromises and ruthlessness. This is undoubtedly true of all politicians; John F. Kennedy spoke of passing the torch to a new generation, and Ronald Reagan waxed lyrical about a shining city on a hill, but both were willing to crush an opponent or cut an unsavory deal when necessary.

The book that follows is the product of months of work by a team of Chicago Tribune reporters. Many have covered Chicago and Illinois politics for years or even decades, providing often-overlooked insights into a figure who is new to much of the country. These journalists conducted hundreds of interviews, including several with Obama himself; visited Indonesia and Hawaii, Washington state and Washington, D.C.; studied numerous documents; and logged many miles with the Obama campaign. The strongest, most consistent theme emerging from the reporting is the tension between Obama's idealism and his pragmatism. This does not necessarily mean that Obama's tactics contradict his message. But like many politicians, he is a complex figure, and the relationship between his public image and his private actions is equally complicated.

For example, Obama seems to have taken liberties with some of the stories of his childhood and youth, depicting a compelling struggle with racial identity that is at odds with the memory of others who were there. When Obama was an organizer in Chicago, his work was defined by careful pragmatism, not sweeping idealism. His first campaign, for state Senate in 1996, showed a willingness to use tough tactics to dispose of his Democratic rivals. Obama carefully plotted his rise to power during his time in the Illinois legislature, voting "present" on some controversial measures, apparently to minimize political risk. In the U.S. Senate, he refused to take a leadership role on some of the emotional issues that had catapulted him to prominence, like his opposition to the Iraq War. In recent years Obama was involved in a real estate deal with a Chicago power broker who was under an ethical cloud. And after securing the Democratic nomination, Obama quickly moved toward the center, edging away from the more liberal positions that helped him win the primary battle.

All typical politics, perhaps. But so much of Obama's message has been that he is beyond typical politics.

And in some ways he is. Because of him, Americans for the first time can envision a specific African-American taking on the powers, trappings and rituals of the presidency. They know that soon a black man may be sitting in the Oval Office, receiving briefings from the director of national intelligence, delivering the State of the Union address to a joint session of Congress, giving orders to five-star generals, holding news conferences in the White House, greeting world leaders in foreign palaces.

In the souvenir stores around Washington, tourists can buy any number of bookmarks, mugs and other trinkets depicting the 43 U.S. presidents, their pictures aligned in stern rows. The sameness of their pale visages is obvious. A much different face may soon appear alongside them. The earliest presidents owned blacks as slaves; now one may join their ranks. Even the possibility is a momentous shift in the current of American history.

The White House has been home to Thomas Jefferson, Abraham Lincoln and Franklin Roosevelt. The nation is seriously contemplating making the next occupant the son of a goat-herding father from Kenya. That mere contemplation may be his great accomplishment, and our stumbling advance.

1 *"A mind in full tilt": His roots*

ON JULY 9, 1896, a little-known former congressman from Nebraska rose to address the Democratic National Convention in Chicago. Few expected anything out of the ordinary. William Jennings Bryan's sole government experience consisted of two terms in the U.S. House of Representatives, and calling him a dark horse overstated his status at the convention. For his speech, Bryan seized on a cause that resonated powerfully with workers and farmers: the free coinage of silver and the rejection of gold as the sole backing for currency.

Bryan proceeded, over the next hour, to arouse the crowd into a frenzy with populist denunciations of banks and corporations, saving his greatest passion for the finale: "We shall answer their demands for a gold standard by saying to them, 'You shall not press down upon the brow of labor this crown of thorns! You shall not crucify mankind upon a cross of gold!'" Bryan then took a step back, extending his arms as though crucified himself, and held the pose for several seconds as the roars of the crowd washed over him. In a time of economic anxiety, the speech released a pent-up stress among the delegates, who became almost delirious. "The floor of the convention seemed to heave up," reported The New York World. "Everybody seemed to go mad at once. The whole face of the convention was broken by the tumult—hills and valleys of shrieking men and women." The next day, Bryan was nominated for president despite his tender age of 36.

A half-century later, at another convention, another young man extolled another controversial cause. Minneapolis Mayor Hubert Humphrey, 37, was frustrated at the lukewarm civil rights plank in the Democratic Party's rambling 1948 platform. Against the wishes of party leaders, and in the

Obama, then a candidate for the U.S. Senate, entered the national stage in July 2004 at the Democratic National Convention in Boston.

face of deep hostility from Southern Democrats, Humphrey rose to demand more at the Democratic convention in Philadelphia. "To those who say that we are rushing this issue of civil rights, I say to them we are 172 years late," Humphrey thundered. "To those who say that this civil rights program is an infringement on states' rights, I say this: The time has arrived in America for the Democratic Party to get out of the shadows of states' rights and to walk forthrightly into the bright sunshine of human rights!" Humphrey's words jolted the delegates from their complacency. Improbably, they adopted a tougher civil rights plank, prompting many Southerners to walk out. Humphrey instantly became a leader of the liberal movement, a status he was to hold for decades.

These are the exceptions. Only a few times in history has a speech sprung a little-known figure into the top rank of American politics. But it happened again in 2004, at yet another Democratic convention, when the party's nominee, Sen. John Kerry of Massachusetts, unexpectedly chose Barack Obama, the U.S. Senate candidate from Illinois, to deliver the keynote address. Obama had received some attention in recent weeks, since he was positioned to become the Senate's only black member, but he was hardly a household name. Kerry had met Obama a few months earlier at a fundraiser in Chicago, where he was struck by Obama's presence and charisma. When Louis Susman, a top Kerry fundraiser, mused, "This guy will be on a national ticket

Obama's grandfather Stanley Dunham (center), back from World War II, holds his infant daughter, who was named Stanley Ann.

someday," Kerry had responded, "I have a way in mind for him to be at the national convention this year." Kerry also had a more practical reason for inviting Obama to deliver the keynote: Kerry had been criticized for poor outreach to black voters, and a starring convention role for Obama could help repair those relations.

And so, on July 27, 2004, the country was introduced to Barack Obama. Obama recognized that this was his first big moment on the national stage, and he seized it. With resonance and sweep, he laid out the themes that were to animate his presidential campaign four years later, though at the time the notion that he might be the next Democratic nominee was inconceivable. "The pundits like to slice and dice our country into red states and blue states; red states for Republicans, blue states for Democrats," Obama said. "But I've got news for them too. We worship an awesome God in the blue states, and we don't like federal agents poking around in our libraries in the red states." He spoke with a rhythmic eloquence that has become familiar but at the time was a revelation, and his theme, then as now, was unity. "There is not a liberal America and a conservative America, there is the United States of America!" Obama declared, as delegates

yelled and jabbed placards with his name into the air. "There is not a black America and a white America and Latino America and Asian America, there's the United States of America!"

The reaction was immediate. CNN's Jeff Greenfield said the address was "one of the really great keynote speeches of the last quarter-century." On MSNBC, Chris Matthews agreed. "That is an amazing moment in history right there," Matthews said. "It is surely an amazing moment. A keynoter like I've never heard." The general response was summed up in The New York Times in terms reminiscent of the reaction to William Jennings Bryan. "Barack Obama owned the town," it reported. "His words of unity and hope brought some to tears and many to loud and long cheers. Some political consultants said it was the best keynote address they had heard in years. And suddenly, on Wednesday, Mr. Obama could not walk around town without being swarmed."

It was perhaps the pivotal moment in Obama's career. He went from relative obscurity to political stardom in the course of an hour. Yet such a scene seemed impossibly distant 43 years earlier, on Aug. 4, 1961, when a boy was born to an African student and his American

Stanley Ann, with parents Stanley and Madelyn Dunham.

wife in Honolulu and they settled on the name Barack, meaning "blessed."

Still, some of the qualities that led Barack Obama to his great moment were visible in his mother, a quick-witted, iconoclastic woman who had grown up hell-bent on resisting Eisenhower-era conformity. Her name was Stanley Ann Dunham, so called because her father had wanted a boy so badly that he named her after himself. As a candidate, Obama would frequently depict the story of his mother, who died of cancer in 1995, as a quintessential tale of the American heartland. In this telling, Ann is a white woman from the flatlands of Kansas, the only daughter of parents who grew up in the "dab-smack, landlocked center of the country." Implicit is this message: If you have any lingering questions about the black candidate with the funny name, just remember that his mother hails from the good earth of Middle America. It's Obama's version of the log cabin story or Bill Clinton's "man from Hope," a validation of his essential American qualities. As it happens, Ann Dunham's formative years were spent not on the Great Plains but more than 1,800 miles away on a small island in the Pacific Northwest. She spent 8th grade through

high school in Washington state, mostly on Mercer Island, a 5-mile-long stretch of Douglas firs and cedars on Lake Washington, just across from Seattle.

Ann's mother, Madelyn Payne, had been raised in the oil boomtown of Augusta, Kansas, by stern Methodist parents who did not believe in drinking, playing cards or dancing. She was one of the best students in her graduating class. And in ways that foretold the flouting of conventions by her daughter Ann, Madelyn rejected her parents' rules, happily making forays to a dance hall in Wichita to listen to big bands led by Benny Goodman, Tommy Dorsey, Glenn Miller and the other stars who came through in those years.

Madelyn met her husband before she had even graduated high school. Four years older, Stanley Armour Dunham—gregarious, friendly, challenging and loud—lived 17 miles away, in El Dorado. Those who knew Dunham described him as a natural salesman "who could charm the legs off a couch." Although Madelyn was far quieter, the attraction was instant. The couple secretly wed in 1940, several weeks before Madelyn's graduation; she did not tell her parents of her wedding until she got her diploma in June, and the news was not well-received in the Payne family home. The marriage of Stanley and Madelyn spanned the railroad tracks, and the general view was that Stanley, who came from a blue-collar background, was on the wrong side of this divide. When World War II came, Stanley enlisted in the Army, while Madelyn worked at Boeing's B-29 production plant in Wichita. Stanley and Madelyn Dunham were to play an enormous role in the life of their grandson Barack Obama, helping raise him and shape his attitudes.

After their only child, Stanley Ann Dunham, arrived in 1942, Stanley managed a furniture store for a few years and Madelyn worked in restaurants, while both restlessly looked for the next opportunity. In 1955 the family moved to Seattle, where Stanley had gotten a job at a bigger store downtown, Standard-Grunbaum Furniture. They soon moved again, this time to nearby Mercer Island, to be closer to a new high school for Ann, who was by now 13. Mercer Island, today a pricey home to corporate luminaries such as Microsoft co-founder Paul Allen, was at the time a rural, idyllic place where children held summer sleepovers along the water. The island was quiet, politically conservative and all white.

"NOT A STANDARD-ISSUE GIRL"

Still, consistent with the 1950s, undercurrents were stirring. In 1955, the chairman of the Mercer Island School Board, John Stenhouse, testified before the House Un-American Activities Committee that he had been a member of the Communist Party. At Mercer Island High School, two teachers, Val Foubert and Jim Wichterman, provoked regular parental thunderstorms by teaching their students to challenge societal norms and question all manner of authority. Foubert taught English, and his texts were cutting-edge: "Atlas Shrugged," "The Organization Man," "The Hidden Persuaders," "1984" and the acerbic writings of H.L. Mencken.

Wichterman taught philosophy, including such challenging thinkers as Sartre and Kierkegaard. Students called the hallway between his classroom and Foubert's "anarchy alley." Wichterman openly violated the norms of the 1950s by questioning the existence of God, and he didn't stop there. "I had them read 'The Communist Manifesto,' and the parents went nuts," Wichterman recalled. Some students began questioning the social pillars of religious tradition, political conservatism and parental authority, a development that outraged their families. Most parents did not believe high school teachers should be discussing sex or religion with their children, and in periodic protests known as "mothers' marches," they pushed to have Wichterman and Foubert fired. Stanley and Madelyn Dunham did not join in the uproar.

Barack Obama Sr. and Stanley Ann Dunham, Barack's parents.

If anything, they seemed to be moving away from the traditionalism of their upbringing and began attending services at nearby East Shore Unitarian Church, sometimes called "the little Red church on the hill" for its leftist leanings.

This was the setting for Ann's upbringing. Boyish and sharp-tongued, Ann had a restless mind. Prone to rolling her eyes when she heard something she disagreed with, she did not like her nose, worried about her weight and complained about her parents. Her sarcasm could be withering and, while she enjoyed arguing, she did not like to draw attention to herself. "She was not a standard-issue girl of her times," said classmate Chip Wall, who went on to teach philosophy. "She wasn't part of the matched-sweater-set crowd." After school, Wall and Dunham would take off to Seattle's coffee shops, where they would discuss philosophy and politics for hours. Maxine Box, Ann's best friend, remembered how unconventional her thinking was. "She touted herself as an atheist, and it was something she'd read about and could argue," Box said. "She was always challenging and arguing and comparing. She was already thinking about things that the rest of us hadn't." While her girlfriends regularly baby-sat, for example, Ann showed no interest in such activities. She made it clear she felt no need to marry or have children, hardly a typical attitude for girls in the late 1950s. Classmate Susan Blake said of her friend, "Hers was a mind in full tilt."

The teachings of Foubert and Wichterman affirmed for Ann that there was life beyond high school dances, football games and slumber parties. The Mercer Island High School Class of 1960 fell between well-defined generations. The Beat generation had passed, and the 1960s era of protest was yet to begin. Students felt they were on the cusp of social change, and they heard the distant early rumblings of the coming struggles over civil rights, women's liberation and war. "If you were concerned about something going wrong in the world, Stanley would know about it first," said Wall, who described her as "a fellow traveler. ... We were liberals before we knew what liberals were." Another classmate, Jill Burton-Dascher, said Ann "was intellectually way more mature than we were and a little bit ahead of her time, in an off-center way."

When the Mercer Island High School yearbooks began circulating in the spring of 1960, Ann's senior year, classmates scribbled their thoughts on the future, slumber parties, one mother's exceptionally good chocolate cake and a group of goofy boys. Dunham wrote to Maxine Box: "Remember me when you are old and gray. Love & Luck, Stanley." Seemingly out of the blue, her father had found a better opportunity—another furniture store, this one in Hawaii. "He just couldn't settle," Box said.

That was only the first surprise. Ann began classes at the University of Hawaii in 1960, and shortly after that, Box received a letter saying her friend had fallen in love with a graduate student. He was from Kenya and his name was Obama.

About the same time, another letter crossed the Pacific, this one heading to Africa. It was from Barack Obama Sr. to his stepmother, Sarah Hussein Onyango Obama. Although the letter didn't go into great detail, it said he had met a young woman named Ann. There wasn't much on how they met or what the attraction was, but he announced their plans to wed.

The Dunhams were not happy, but Ann's prospective father-in-law was furious, writing the Dunhams a harsh letter declaring his disapproval of the marriage. "He didn't want the Obama blood sullied by a white woman," Obama Jr. recounted in his first book, "Dreams from My Father." But parental objections mattered little to the young couple. For Ann, her relationship with Barack Obama was an extension of the long coffeehouse sessions in Seattle and the teachings of Wichterman and Foubert. The couple spent weekends listening to jazz, drinking beer and debating politics and world affairs with other University of Hawaii graduate students. Neil Abercrombie, now a Democratic congressman from Hawaii, who was part of those gatherings, remembered the senior Obama as self-assured, opinionated and possessed of a voice so deep "he made James Earl Jones

seem like a tenor."

A FATHER LEAVES

While Obama was impatient and energized, Ann was patient and quietly passionate in her arguments. She was the only woman in the group. "I think she was attracted to his powerful personality," Abercrombie said. "And he was attracted to her beauty and her calmness."

Six months after they wed, another letter arrived in Kenya, announcing the birth of Barack Hussein Obama.

Despite her husband's continued anger, Sarah Obama said later that she "was so happy to have a grandchild in the U.S." But when the news hit Mercer Island, it dumbfounded Ann's classmates. At the time of her graduation just a year earlier, she had been pointedly uninterested in marriage or motherhood. Although he didn't say it at the time, Abercrombie privately feared the relationship would be short-lived. Obama was one of the most ambitious, self-focused men he had ever met. When Obama was accepted to study at Harvard, Ann did not accompany him, and she disappeared from the University of Hawaii student gatherings.

"I know he loved Ann," Abercrombie said. But "I think he didn't want the impediment of being responsible for a family. He expected great things of himself, and he was going off to achieve them." Ann filed for divorce in 1964. The senior Obama finished his work at Harvard and returned to Kenya, where he hoped to realize his dream of playing a prominent role in the newly independent government of Jomo Kenyatta. His father's abandonment would become a major theme for the younger Obama. Years after Obama Sr. left Hawaii, Abercrombie and another friend from graduate school looked up their old pal on a trip through Africa. At that point, the elder Obama was a bitter man, according to the congressman, feeling that he had been denied due opportunities to influence the running of his country. "He was drinking too much. His frustration was apparent," Abercrombie said. To Abercrombie's surprise, Obama never asked about his son.

2 *"A race thing": The early years*

HAWAII WAS A TROUBLED, unsettled place in 1961. It had become a state just two years earlier, and many native Hawaiians were deeply unhappy about that. The U.S. military was expanding on the island of Oahu, home to the new capital of Honolulu. But the perpetually smiling boy the family called Barry was oblivious to all this. In snapshots, he is the epitome of childhood bliss. He played on the beach. He posed in lifeguard stands. He rode a bright blue tricycle with red, white and blue streamers dangling from the handlebars. Raising a mixed-race child in the early 1960s was hardly a conventional exercise in an America still years away from the Civil Rights Act and the assassination of Martin Luther King. But if there was a place where it was less unorthodox, less a violation of convention, that place was Hawaii, where mixed-race children were not uncommon among the highly diverse population.

Obama's mother was 18 when he was born, and her husband abandoned her a short time later to study at Harvard University. So it was natural that Obama's grandparents would step in. In essence he was raised by three people—his mother, Ann, his grandfather Stanley and his grandmother Madelyn. Neil Abercrombie, a family friend, frequently saw young Obama around town with his grandfather, whom Obama called Gramps. "Stanley loved that little boy," Abercrombie said. "In the absence of his father, there was not a kinder, more understanding man than Stanley Dunham." Years later, at Obama's wedding reception in Chicago, Obama brought the crowd to tears when he spoke of his recently deceased maternal grandfather and how he made a little boy with an absent father feel as though he was never alone. Madelyn, then a rising executive at the Bank of Hawaii,

Ann with son Barack in Hawaii shortly after Barack Obama Sr. had left the two to pursue his studies at Harvard University.

Young Barack plays on the beach with his grandfather Stanley Dunham.

Barack in the 1960s in Hawaii.

"He liked drawing Spider-Man and Batman. Barry liked to draw heroes."

Obama friend Widiyanto Hendro Cahyono

was more reserved, but she relished having her grandson's friends over to play. "Those were robust years, full of energy and cacophony, and she loved all of it," Obama's half-sister, Maya Soetoro-Ng, said of her grandmother. Ann and Barack lived with the Dunhams in Honolulu until Obama was 6. Then Ann got married again, this time to an Indonesian student, Lolo Soetoro, who was studying at the University of Hawaii. In one family photo before the mother and son moved to Indonesia with Lolo, Obama walked barefoot on Waikiki Beach, his arms outstretched as though embracing the entire beautiful life around him. A sailboat called the Manu Kai—"bird of the sea"—was about to set sail behind him.

THE QUEST TO BELONG

Obama, too, was about to journey far from familiar shores, and not just geographically. Obama would soon develop into a child deeply affected by his father's abandonment, perpetually wrestling with his racial identity, yet somehow able to thrive in greatly disparate worlds. His life stories, as Obama the candidate has told them, have a common theme: the quest to belong. Throughout his youth, especially as depicted in Obama's first book, "Dreams from My Father," he always found ways to meld into even the most unwelcoming communities. And he frequently made peace with the very people who angered him most, sometimes even finding ways to make allies of them.

When discussing his years in Indonesia, Obama has described making friends easily, becoming fluent in Indonesian in just six months and integrating easily into the foreign fabric of Jakarta. The reality was less tidy. When Obama and his mother joined her new husband—a kind man who later would become a heavy drinker and womanizer, according to family members—their Jakarta neighborhood resembled a village more than the bustling metropolis it is today. Electricity had arrived only a few years earlier. Half the homes were old bamboo huts; half, including the Soetoro house, were nicer, with brick or concrete and red-tiled roofs.

Former playmates remember Obama as "Barry Soetoro," or simply "Barry," a chubby little boy. He was teased more than any other kid in the neighborhood, primarily because he was bigger and had black features. He was the only foreign child, and one of the few enrolled in a new Catholic school in an area populated almost entirely by Betawis, an old tribal group whose members practiced a highly traditional Islam. Some of the Betawi children threw rocks at the open Catholic classrooms, remembered Cecilia Sugini Hananto, who taught Obama in 2nd grade. Obama never fully grasped the Indonesian language, according to teachers, former playmates and friends, and he was quiet as a result. One word Obama did learn quickly in his new home was "curang," which means "cheater." When kids teased him, Obama yelled back, "Curang, curang!" When a friend gave him shrimp paste instead of chocolate, he yelled, "Curang, curang!"

Zulfan Adi was one of the neighborhood kids who teased Obama most mercilessly. One day young Obama, a hopelessly upbeat boy who seemed unaware that the older kids didn't want him tagging along, followed a group of Adi's friends to a nearby swamp. "They held his hands and feet and said, 'One, two, three,' and threw him in the swamp," recalled Adi. "Luckily he could swim. They only did it to Barry." Other kids would scrap with him sometimes, but because Obama was bigger and better-fed than many of them, he was hard to defeat. "He was built like a bull. So we'd get three kids together to fight him," recalled Yunaldi Askiar, 45, a former neighborhood friend. "But it was only playing."

Israella Pareira Darmawan, Obama's 1st-grade teacher, attempted to help him learn the Indonesian language by going over pronunciation and vowel sounds. He struggled greatly with the language, and with his studies as a result, and he always sat in the back corner of the classroom. His friends called him "Negro," which was not considered a slur at the time in Indonesia. Still, his teachers recognized leadership qualities in him. "He would be very helpful with friends. He'd pick them up if they fell down," Darmawan recalled. "He would protect the smaller ones." Notably, in an essay on what he wanted to do when he grew up, Obama wrote that he wanted to be president. "He didn't say what country he wanted to be president of," said his 3rd-grade teacher, Fermina Katarina Sinaga. "But he wanted to make everybody happy."

The next year, the Soetoro family moved to a new, more affluent neighborhood that, while just 3 miles to the west, seemed a world away. Elite Dutch colonists once lived there, and the Japanese moved in during their occupation of Indonesia in World War II. In the early 1970s, diplomats and Indonesian businessmen lived there in fancy gated houses with wide paved roads and sculpted

At home in Jakarta, Indonesia, Lolo Soetoro and Ann Dunham with their daughter Maya and Barack.

bushes. Obama never became terribly close with the children of his new school, this time a predominantly Muslim one. As in the old school, Obama sat in a back corner. He sketched American cartoon characters during class. "He liked drawing Spider-Man and Batman," said a friend, Widiyanto Hendro Cahyono. "Barry liked to draw heroes."

Indonesia may be where Obama first consciously confronted the issue of his race. He has told one particular story of a watershed moment in his journey of racial discovery time and again. He was 9, he said, and one day he visited his mother, who was working at the U.S. Embassy in Jakarta. Obama passed the time by looking through several issues of Life magazine, and he came across an article that he later would describe as feeling like an "ambush attack." The piece included photos of a black man who had destroyed his skin with powerful chemical lighteners that promised to make him white. Instead, the chemicals had peeled off much of his skin, leaving him sad and scarred. "I imagine other black children, then and now, undergoing similar moments of revelation," Obama wrote in "Dreams from My Father."

Yet no such Life issue exists, according to historians at the magazine. No such photos, no such article. When asked about the discrepancy, Obama said, "It might have been an Ebony or it might have been ... Who knows what it was?" At the request of the Chicago Tribune, archivists at Ebony searched their past articles, and none of them matched Obama's recollection either. This, of course, doesn't prove that such a magazine article doesn't exist. More to the point is this: Judging from the memories of his childhood friends, it is unlikely that, at age 9, it would have taken a magazine story to jolt Obama into an awareness that his blackness was an issue. As Obama has told the story of his life, particularly his racial self-discovery, to an ever-growing audience, he has sometimes made the story seem clearer than it was, a better narrative, with sharp turning points and well-defined characters. Some of this, no doubt, is the fuzziness of anyone recalling long-ago childhood events. In some cases, Obama's stories have made him look better in the retelling; in others, they have appeared to exaggerate his struggle over issues of race, or simply skimmed over some of the more painful moments.

That is particularly true of his time at Punahou School in Honolulu. Compelling as Indonesia was, Ann was concerned about her son's education, and she decided to move Obama back to Hawaii so he could attend the elite preparatory academy. As he was about to start 5th grade, Ann, Obama and a new baby sister, Maya, moved into a small apartment near the school's sprawling, lush campus. From his first day until his high school graduation in 1979, the young man was one of only a small number of black students at a school heavily populated by the children of Hawaii's wealthy, most of them white and Asian.

"IT COULD BE A LONELY PLACE"

Punahou and Hawaii liked to see themselves as more diverse and colorblind than the rest of the nation. But the reality felt far different to the handful of African-Americans attending classes there. Rik Smith, a black Punahou student 2 years older than Obama, remembered one Halloween when white students dressed as slaves, coming to school in tattered clothes and their faces painted black with shoe polish. "Like being black was a funny costume in and of itself," Smith said. He added, "Punahou was an amazing school, but it could be a lonely place. ... Those of us who were black did feel isolated, there's no question about that." In response, the black boys banded together. "The brothers," as Lewis Anthony Jr., an African-American in the class of 1977 put it, often talked about race and civil rights. They sought out parties away from school, especially at nearby military bases, where other African-Americans would be in attendance.

Obama, however, was not a part of that group, according to Anthony and Smith. Both seemed surprised that in "Dreams," Obama wrote about routinely going to parties at Schofield Barracks and other military bases. "We'd all do things together, but Obama was never there," Smith said. "I went to those parties up at Schofield but never saw him at any of them."

Obama had a large, racially diverse group of friends at Punahou, many of whom would crowd into his grandparents' apartment after school. One of them was Greg Orme, a smart, respectful teenager from a white, middle-class family. Although Orme spent most afternoons with Obama and considered him one of his closest friends, he said Obama never brought up issues of race, never talked about feeling out of place at Punahou. "He never verbalized any of that," Orme said. "He was a very provocative thinker. He would bring up worldly topics far beyond his years. But we never talked race." And when Obama's mother, with her unquenchable wanderlust, announced that she was returning to Indonesia, Obama, then a teenager, asked to stay at Punahou. Once again, he moved in with his grandparents.

One place Obama found a sense of community was on the basketball court. A member of the varsity squad,

Ann, Barack, Maya and grandfather Stanley Dunham in Honolulu after Ann had returned with the children to Hawaii from Indonesia.

though not a starter, Obama helped take Punahou to the state championship in 1979, his senior year. Adept at nailing long jump shots, Obama was called "Barry O'Bomber" by teammates. One of them, Alan Lum, said Obama was always the first to confront coaches when he felt they were not fairly allotting playing time. "He'd go right up to the coach during a game and say, 'Coach, we're killing this team. Our second string should be playing more,'" Lum said. But Obama seemed happiest on the basketball court in the off-season. Punahou had several courts where 20-something men from nearby neighborhoods would come in the late afternoons for what often turned into flashy, competitive pickup sessions. Many of the men were black. "At the time, it

A yearbook photo from 1977 shows Barack Obama with the basketball team at Punahou School in Honolulu. Adept at nailing long jump shots, Obama was called "Barry O'Bomber" by teammates.

"He was a very provocative thinker. He would bring up worldly topics far beyond his years. But we never talked race."

Obama friend Greg Orme

was about basketball," said Orme, who has remained friends with Obama and plays basketball with him almost every Christmas. "But looking back now, I can see he was seeking more from those guys than that. He was probably studying them and learning from them. He was a younger black man looking for guidance."

As he prepared to graduate, Obama, like the other seniors, was given the opportunity to design a quarter-page in the yearbook. The students composed notes to friends and family members and included photos or quotes. On page 271 of the 1979 Oahuan, Obama thanked "Tut" and "Gramps," his nicknames for Madelyn and Stanley Dunham. He also thanked the "Choom Gang," a reference to "chooming," Hawaiian slang for smoking marijuana. Obama admitted in "Dreams" that during high school he frequently smoked marijuana, drank alcohol, even used cocaine occasionally. "Junkie. Pothead. That's where I'd been headed: the final, fatal role of the young would-be black man," Obama wrote.

In the book, which Obama wrote long before he was nationally known, his high school years are described as a time of turbulent, sometimes painful self-discovery, as Obama groped toward a comfortable racial identity. It's hard to know how to interpret the fact that this turmoil was not evident even to his closest friends. There is, of course, no reason to doubt that Obama struggled deeply with racial identity as he was coming of age, regardless of whether that struggle was obvious to his friends. It's possible that in his accounts of that time, Obama has created, consciously or not, external stories to match his inner struggles, in an attempt to clarify and give shape to something that was difficult and often shapeless.

STRUGGLE FOR RACIAL IDENTITY
Obama recounts in "Dreams" his discussions on race and racism with a Punahou student, "Ray," described as perpetually angry at the white world around him. "It's their world, all right," Ray ostensibly shouted at Obama. "They own it and we in it. So just get the fuck outta my face." The real Ray, a man named Keith Kakugawa, is half-black and half-Japanese, and says he always considered himself mixed-race, like many in Hawaii, and was hardly an angry black man. He did recall long, soulful talks with Obama and says his friend confided his longing and loneliness. But Kakugawa is certain that these

sentiments were not about race. "Not even close," he said, adding that Obama was dealing with "some inner turmoil" in those days. "But it wasn't a race thing," he said. "Barry's biggest struggles then were missing his parents. His biggest struggles were his feelings of abandonment. The idea that his biggest struggle was race is bullshit." As for his comment that "It's their world," Kakugawa said Obama's recollection was mistaken. "I did say we were playing in their world, but that had nothing to do with race," he said. "He knew that." What he had meant, Kakugawa said, was that he and Obama were operating in a universe shaped by the powerful people who ran Punahou—famous Hawaiian families like the Doles, owners of the pineapple fortune, or the original developers of Waikiki, the tourist mecca. "It just wasn't a race thing," he reiterated.

In another passage of the book, Obama has Ray complaining that white Punahou girls did not want to date black guys and that he and Obama did not get enough playing time as athletes, and speculating that they would be "treated different if we was white. Or Japanese. Or Hawaiian. Or fucking Eskimo." But Kakugawa, a convicted drug felon, said he has never been the "prototypical angry black guy" Obama portrayed. Because of his biracial heritage, he said, he was "like everyone in Hawaii, a mix of a lot of things." A close friend and track teammate of Kakugawa's, John Hagar, also said he was surprised by Obama's description of the character representing Kakugawa. "I never picked up on that," Hagar said. "He was just one of those perfect [ethnic] mixes of everything you see in Hawaii."

"THAT NIGHT HAD UPSET HIM"
Another story put forth in "Dreams" as a pivotal moment of racial awakening checks out essentially as Obama wrote it. Obama recounted taking two white friends, including Orme, to a party attended almost entirely by African-Americans. In the book, the characters representing Orme and the other friend ask to leave the party after just an hour, saying they feel out of place. The experience, Obama wrote, made him furious, as he realized that whites held a "fundamental power" over blacks. Orme remembered the episode clearly. "One of us said that being the different guys in the room had awakened a little bit of empathy to what he must feel all

Obama graduated from Punahou School in 1979. He was among a small number of black students there.

the time at school. And he clearly didn't appreciate that," Orme said. "I never knew, until reading the book later, how much that night had upset him."

As Obama's senior year drew to a close, his mother sent him letters from afar about her life in Indonesia and her economic development work with non-profit groups there. She also sent advice about his future. College would be his next stop, and Ann mixed encouragement to keep up his grades with laments about American politics. "It is a shame we have to worry so much about [grades], but you know what the college entrance competition is these days," she wrote. "Did you know that in Thomas Jefferson's day, and right up through the 1930s, anybody who had the price of tuition could go to Harvard? ... I don't see that we are producing many Thomas Jeffersons nowadays. Instead we are producing Richard Nixons."

In the spring of 1979, Obama's mother and his half-sister Maya flew to Hawaii for his high school graduation.

If young Obama had struggled to find a place at Punahou, it was well-hidden on this day as he laughed and posed for photos with friends. With a trimmed Afro and Hawaiian leis around his neck, Obama was surrounded by the disparate people who shaped him. In one photo he hugged his beaming sister. In another photo, a striking snapshot with his grandparents, Stanley smiled proudly while Madelyn hugged Obama fiercely, as though she did not want to let him go into a world far from the remote island that had long been his home.

3 *"No permanent friends": College and community organizing*

BARACK OBAMA was barely 18 when he arrived at Occidental College, a small liberal arts school in Los Angeles, and settled into a first-floor room in Haines Hall, with music blasting from stereos and students living as much in the halls as in their rooms. Obama still called himself Barry, and his Occidental days seem to have been, by his own description, a haze of parties, alcohol, illicit drugs and pseudo-radical talk. His mother scolded him for turning into a "good-time Charlie." Clearly he stood out. One classmate, Amiekoleh "Kim" Kimbrew, recalled Obama striding across campus in flip-flops. "He was very popular," she said. "There were rumors that he was a Hawaiian prince."

But somewhere along the line at Occidental,

At Harvard, Obama was the first black president of the Harvard Law Review.

Barry became Barack, and he became more serious — less a fun-loving Hawaiian kid and more a thoughtful activist. Liberalism no doubt came naturally to the son of Ann Dunham, who had always rejected conventionality. Obama's social activism was largely limited to coffeehouse talk, but he did help plan a large campus rally demanding that the college divest from South Africa, a popular cause on college campuses at the time. Obama opened the rally with a bit of street theater, speaking for a few minutes until two white students in paramilitary dress dragged him away. His performance caught the attention of Rebecca Rivera, another rally participant. "I wonder why he isn't more politically active on campus," Rivera thought. She made a mental note to "try to get him involved."

"HIS OPINION WAS RESPECTED"
At Oxy, as students called it, Obama, true to form, bridged the gap between student groups. In "Dreams from My Father," Obama took a gently self-mocking tone, writing that he hung out not just with black students but with "the foreign students. The Chicanos. The Marxist professors and structural feminists and punk-rock performance poets. ... When we ground out our cigarettes in the hallway carpet or set our stereos so loud that the walls began to shake, we were resisting bourgeois society's stifling constraints." He spent time with the pizza crowd at Casa Bianca and with the lefties at The Cooler, an on-campus snack bar and coffeehouse whose denizens were referred to as Cooler Marxists. Kenneth Sulzer, who lived in Obama's dorm, remembered long discussions about politics, the Soviet invasion of Afghanistan and a possible reinstitution of the draft. "We ate pizza, hung out, drank beer," Sulzer said. Obama, Sulzer added, was "relatively quiet. But when he spoke, his opinion was respected. He was not a shouter or screamer. He was on the thoughtful side, even at that age."

But after two years, Obama wanted something more. He wearied of the parties, and his mother's warnings began to take hold. He transferred to Columbia University in New York City. In his book, he says he was seeking a more urban experience and a degree in political science, but the move also reflected a shift toward intellectual maturity and a more sober outlook. His time at Columbia was quieter and more anonymous than his time at Occidental. He read a lot, and only a handful of fellow students remembered him. Those who did described him as more likely to hit the library than the bars. "If I had to give one adjective to describe him, it is mature," said William Araiza, who took an international politics class with Obama. "He was our age but seemed older because of his poise." A professor named Michael L. Baron, who taught a seminar on international relations, gave Obama an A for a paper on

U.S.-Soviet disarmament talks. "It was a great class — all seniors, and they were all intensively studying issues such as the Cuban Missile Crisis, the Middle East," Baron said. "He was a very earnest student who always participated in the classroom discussion."

After his graduation in 1983, Obama worked briefly for a New York financial consultant and then a consumer organization. But he was restless, and he began looking for something more satisfying. On a trip to the New York Public Library, Obama was scanning a newsletter when he spotted an ad from an Illinois group seeking an African-American to organize a dozen black churches in Chicago. The idea was to help community members develop tactics to influence politicians, to help the disadvantaged learn to wield power. Intrigued, Obama sent in his résumé.

The man who received it was a rumpled, soft-spoken activist. Gerald Kellman hoped to mobilize the churches — the most solid organizations in many poorer neighborhoods — to fight the fallout from the rapid decline of Chicago's steel industry. But Kellman and his organizer buddy Mike Kruglik were both white and Jewish, and some black church members couldn't warm up to them. So Kellman shifted Kruglik to the suburbs and was looking for someone to replace him. Kellman wanted an African-American, but the résumé he received was from a Hawaiian native with a strange name. "'Obama'—is that Japanese?" Kellman asked his Japanese-American wife. "Actually, it could be," she answered. Kellman had plans to visit family in New York, so he called Obama and set up an interview. They met at a coffee shop on the Upper West Side, and Kellman quickly began testing Obama with pointed questions. Why would someone with Obama's potential want to go into a field as unglamorous as organizing? "He said he wanted to make fundamental change," Kellman said. "He wanted to make it from the grass roots, and he wanted to learn." Kellman hired Obama on the spot for roughly $10,000 a year, throwing in an extra $2,000 for a car.

GOING INTO A BATTLE ZONE
Community organizing has long attracted socially conscious young people, with its goal of empowering the poor and disenfranchised. Saul Alinsky, the godfather of professional organizing, used Chicago as his lab. Alinsky began his work in the Back of the Yards neighborhood during the Great Depression, persuading hostile groups of white ethnics to band together to pressure meatpackers and slumlords for better conditions. He later took his tactics to Chicago's black neighborhoods, and to other cities as well. Thanks to Alinsky, would-be organizers considered Chicago something of a mecca.

Obama packed his few belongings into a creaky old

Honda and headed into the political and social battle zone that was Chicago in the mid-1980s. Obama knew little of the city's power structure, its social fabric or its political machine. When the 23-year-old arrived in 1985, the racially charged fighting between Harold Washington, the city's first black mayor, and white ethnic aldermen led by Ed Vrdolyak had earned the city a bitter nickname—Beirut on the Lake. "Barack had to learn real estate and insurance and mortgage banking and all the scams of the world," Kellman said. "He had to learn Chicago ward politics and the relationship between graft and public life." At the same time, Obama felt inspired by Washington, who was providing the city's African-Americans with a feeling of hope and power they had never had.

The rookie organizer was half the age of those he was supposed to help, and many called him "Baby-Face Obama." It became a term of endearment, though, as Obama's poise gained their respect. "The guy was just totally comfortable with who he was and where he was," said John Owens, a community member whom Obama eventually hired as an assistant. Shortly after his arrival, at a meeting with community leaders, Obama acknowledged his inexperience. "I know you all think I'm a young whippersnapper," he said. "Let me set your fears to rest. We're going to learn together." On long walks, Kellman gave Obama the basics. In the Alinsky school of organizing, power was a cherished concept, and it came from two sources: organized money and organized people. But organizers were not supposed to set the agenda. Their role was to probe and find out what community members wanted. So Obama was to conduct 20 to 30 in-depth interviews a week.

Rev. Alvin Love, pastor of Lilydale First Baptist Church, was accustomed to having strangers ask for handouts. When Love opened his door one day in 1985, he assumed that's what the lanky young man was up to. "Who is this skinny guy, and what does he want?" Love wondered. But Obama was looking for Love's thoughts, not his money. "He asked what I wanted to see get done and what was important in this neighborhood," Love said. Obama's interest impressed the 28-year-old minister, who had been looking for ways to connect his aging congregation with a surrounding neighborhood that was getting younger and rougher. But the core of Obama's group, called the Developing Communities Project, was formed by middle-age women like Loretta Augustine Herron. He had grown up apart from his mother for much of his youth, and at DCP he was surrounded by surrogate mothers. He coached them in the skills they would need to confront bureaucrats and politicians; they complained that he ate like a bird and needed to lighten up. Herron appointed herself Obama's fashion adviser, telling him what matched and

what didn't. "You shouldn't be so somber and uptight and serious all the time," she told him. He replied, "Yeah, but I'm doing serious work." Obama worked out of a cramped office at Holy Rosary Church, which he shared with Kellman and Kruglik, who acted as sounding boards for the young organizer. From the beginning, Obama brought a decidedly practical view. He did not see the battles between Washington and Vrdolyak as good versus evil, as many in the black community did. "They're not enemies," Obama would say. "They're both working for their constituents, and they have to do this. Whoever can help you reach your goal, that's who you work with. ... There are no permanent friends, no permanent enemies."

DELIBERATE AND METICULOUS

Obama's years as an activist were his first extended experience in the adult world, and the lessons he absorbed were pragmatic ones — try to befriend everyone, use your charm, create alliances, don't ally yourself too strongly with any one camp. The art of working with one's enemies came straight out of his training at the Roseland community and the Altgeld Gardens public housing development. The goal was not sweeping change but modest steps. Obama's hallmark was meticulous planning. Before encounters with public officials, he had community members rehearse possible scenarios over and over to minimize surprises. The group's board meetings dragged on for hours. There was a meeting before the meeting to map out what was to be discussed. Then there was the meeting. Then there was the meeting after the meeting to critique how it went.

Obama's deliberateness even played a role in his decision about where to worship. His group, DCP, was based in churches, and some grumbled that he didn't have a church of his own. Obama, whose mother was decidedly non-religious, eventually settled on Trinity United Church of Christ, a congregation with an activist minister named Rev. Jeremiah Wright Jr. — a decision that would have enormous ramifications two decades later. Wright was an intellectual as well as a pastor, and Trinity provided a solid connection with the African-American community, something Obama may have been seeking. But part of its appeal was more basic — it wasn't affiliated with DCP. "If I joined one of the churches I was already organizing, that might have caused some tensions," Obama said. "And part of it was, there was an explicitly political aspect to the mission and message of Trinity at that time that I found appealing."

Wherever he went, Obama scribbled and doodled. The margins of his notepads were filled with sketches of people he met. Sometimes he drew them laughing, sometimes smiling, sometimes with pointy heads. As part of his training, Obama was expected to take copious notes about his interactions, but he had another motive for jotting everything down. "I want to be a writer," Obama told a friend one day. "These are for a book I plan to write." At night, Obama would hole up in his apartment and craft short stories, basing his characters on people and situations he encountered in Roseland. None of that fiction was ever published. He lived sparingly. Obama's mother teased him about having just two of everything— two plates, two towels. His main indulgences were a cat, Max, and his eclectic library. Volumes on black power were stuffed next to books on Karl Marx, the writings of conservative economist Milton Friedman and a biography of Robert Moses, the ruthless New York City planning czar.

Not that Obama was a monk. He played pickup basketball with fervor, and he gradually developed a social circle. There were girlfriends, including one he lived with for a while. But organizing remained his focus. Altgeld Gardens, the development where he spent much of his time, was surrounded by waste dumps and industrial brownfields. In 1986, it was also the center of a dramatic protest, in which Obama was deeply involved, over delays in clearing asbestos from the apartments. But the more he worked as an organizer, the more he became convinced that the most serious problems could not be solved on a local level. "People were still poor, kids were out on the corner selling drugs, schools weren't working," he said. His frustration was, paradoxically, amplified by Mayor Washington's popularity in the black community. Washington was more attentive to the needs of the heavily African-American South Side than his white predecessors had been, but city services were still lacking, and rallying people to fight City Hall is hard when the mayor is their hero. When Washington died in late 1987, the fight to replace him discouraged many in the African-American community.

Obama yearned to do something on a bigger stage, he told Kellman. Maybe he should go to law school and enter politics. Two years into Obama's time in Chicago, he and Kellman attended a conference at Harvard University. Strolling the same ivy-covered campus his father had left his family to attend more than two decades earlier, Obama reflected on a lesson from his father's life. The elder Obama had returned to his native Kenya bursting with intellect and ambition, only to become embittered because he couldn't reconcile his ideals with political reality. Obama was determined not to fall into that trap. "He talked about what happens to you if you're not practical in finding ways to do things effectively," Kellman said. Obama's resignation months later to attend Harvard Law School didn't shock DCP members. "We always knew he was not ours to keep," Herron said.

As he said his goodbyes in Chicago, Obama told acquaintances that a law degree would let him press for change more effectively. He confided to a fellow organizer that he wanted to someday follow Washington as Chicago mayor. But first he had to get to Massachusetts. He found a used Datsun 210 hatchback that a police officer was selling for $500. It was bright yellow, with rust spots and a hole in the floor, and Obama thought it resembled an overripe banana. But it ran, and it managed to get Obama from Chicago's South Side to Harvard's elegant campus.

The transition must have been jarring, even for a young man accustomed to abrupt changes of scenery. In his late 20s, Obama was older than many of his Harvard classmates and had seen more of life. Intellectually and emotionally, he was ready for Harvard. He could soon be seen around campus sporting a bomber jacket and jeans, a cigarette dangling from his fingers. He excelled academically, and he wasted little time engaging Harvard's formidable professors in argument. "He had a mature approach—he wasn't interested in a debate for debate's sake," said his classmate Cassandra Butts, who would remain a close friend. "He really wanted to see the other person's side of the argument. That didn't mean he was backing away from his position or not staying true to his values." Another classmate, Steve Heinen, recalled, "He was politically more liberal than I am, so I wasn't necessarily agreeing with him in class. But he was always very articulate and well-spoken. Some classmates were militant; he was very level-headed." Gina Torielli, who was in a study group with Obama, had a similar memory. "About once a week we would talk about what we wanted to do [in the future], and Barack was the only person from our class who was interested in government service from the beginning," Torielli said. "He was thinking about public policy while most of us were thinking about getting a paying job."

What ultimately elevated Obama beyond merely being a very impressive law student was his tenure as president of the Harvard Law Review. His academic performance had qualified him for the Review, and after he became an editor he was eligible to run for president. The process was infused with ritual. Voting took place in a building with cooking facilities, and all the candidates brought food to cook for the current Law Review editors as they chose their successors. After a series of votes, Obama won when the publication's conservatives, a vocal minority, threw their support to him. Obama was an unabashed liberal, but the conservatives believed he was most likely to take their perspective into account. Heading the Harvard Law Review was a premier achievement for any aspiring lawyer, perhaps equaled only by a Supreme Court clerkship. Obama, then 28, was the first African-

Obama at Columbia University. His grandparents, Stanley and Madelyn Dunham, had come to New York to visit him. He graduated in 1983.

American ever to be chosen, and news organizations across the country took notice, including the Chicago Tribune, the newspaper of his adopted hometown. "Activist in Chicago now heads Harvard Law Review," announced a Tribune headline on Feb. 7, 1990. The laudatory story added, "For Obama, it's another victory in the fight against 'powerlessness.'"

But getting elected was only the beginning. Obama had to manage some of the most brilliant, and egotistical, legal minds in the country, since the Law Review published articles by high-powered professors as well as students. Ultimately the job was political as much as scholarly. "You have a group of high achievers," said Thomas Perrelli, who worked with Obama. "One of the reasons he was elected was the general sense that he would give everybody, no matter their view, an equal shake. He tried to build consensus. ... You have to have incredible diplomacy, you have to have tremendous analytical skills. Barack was

tremendous. He had the toughness to work with professors to improve their pieces without doing what a lot of Law Review editors do, go overboard. He had a deft touch to work with people to make them feel like they had something to contribute."

Despite the headiness of his success at the nation's top law school, Obama never wavered in his determination to return to Chicago. Despite having lived in Hawaii, Indonesia, California, New York and Cambridge, he had decided Chicago was his hometown. He told the Tribune that after getting his law degree he would probably spend a couple of years practicing law and then return to community organizing or jump into politics. "I'll definitely be coming back to Chicago," he said. "Chicago's a great town ... an ideal laboratory."

4 *"Knock them all over": The path to politics*

OBAMA RETURNED TO CHICAGO with a renewed sense of confidence and ambition. He had starred at Harvard Law School, the country's most prestigious academic institution, and if he'd had any doubts about his ability to perform on a national stage, they were likely gone. With local credibility from his organizing days, national credentials from Harvard and personal aspirations to make a mark, it was only a matter of time before he jumped into politics. Obama nurtured a quiet ambition to someday follow the inspirational Harold Washington as mayor of Chicago, and he had told a Harvard classmate that his dream job was to be governor of Illinois. That, at the time, was the scope of his ambition—to win a prominent role in Illinois politics. As it happened, the opportunity for political office was to come along relatively soon, provided by one of the city's more spectacular sex scandals.

But first, Obama, then 34, settled comfortably into Chicago's South Side. Initially he continued on the path of activism, running Project Vote, a group that registered tens of thousands of black Chicagoans with the help of volunteers whose T-shirts proclaimed, "It's a power thing." The effort played a part in Bill Clinton's success in capturing Illinois, and a bigger role in Carol Moseley Braun's historic 1992 election that made her the first black woman in the U.S. Senate.

But soon Obama's life grew more comfortable, more stable, more mature. Several years earlier, he had met a woman named Michelle Robinson, who was his adviser when he was a summer associate at the Chicago law firm Sidley Austin during law school. Obama was immediately intrigued by Robinson, but Robinson was initially uninterested in dating him, having made a

Michelle and Barack Obama on their wedding day,
Oct. 3, 1992, in Chicago.

promise to avoid boyfriends and focus on herself. "I'm
your adviser," she had told Obama. "Certainly that's going
to look bad. That's just way too predictable." She added,
"[We are] the only two black people here, and [we're]
going to start dating?" Robinson had gone so far as to try
to set him up with other women. But Obama was
persistent, and eventually he persuaded Robinson. On
Oct. 3, 1992, the two got married, with community
organizers packing their wedding at Trinity United
Church of Christ. The newlyweds bought a condo in
Hyde Park, the socially and politically active
neighborhood that includes the University of Chicago.
Obama began working at a small but influential law firm,
teaching constitutional law and sitting on the boards
of charities. But what he was really doing was
biding his time.

These were the years, the early 1990s, when Mayor
Richard M. Daley consolidated his power in Chicago,
establishing a hold over city politics that would rival that
of his legendary father. First elected in 1989, Daley won

re-election in 1991 by an almost 50 percentage-point
margin, along with a sizable City Council majority.
He remapped the city's wards, doing all he could
to fragment the political clout of the city's African-
Americans, striving to avoid a repeat of Washington's rise
to power years earlier on the shoulders of a unified black
community. Before long, it was difficult for any politician
to make headway in the city without first winning Daley's
approval and becoming part of his network. On the state
level, meanwhile, Illinois remained solidly Republican,
as the GOP routinely won support not only from
downstate rural voters but also the suburban counties
that ringed Chicago.

In all, not the easiest political landscape for a novice
to break into. But the eruption of a classic, if tawdry,
politics-and-sex scandal presented the young lawyer with
an opening he wasted no time seizing. In August 1994,
Chicago Congressman Mel Reynolds called a bizarre
press conference to announce that he was under
investigation for having sex with a teenager who had
worked in his campaign office, while angrily denying the
charges and calling the girl an "emotionally disturbed
nutcase." The subsequent trial was a distasteful drama, as
prosecutors played tapes of Reynolds having sexually
explicit phone conversations with Beverly Heard, who
was 16 when she worked in his office. Reynolds insisted
they had only had phone sex, but the jury did not find
that credible, and on Aug. 22, 1995, Reynolds was
convicted of sex crimes and obstruction of justice.

Reynolds' resignation set up a special election for his
congressional seat. Among those who jumped into the
race was Alice Palmer, a longtime activist then serving in
the state Senate. And she made it clear she liked the idea
of Obama as a successor for her Illinois Senate seat.

A DISTRICT WITH HISTORY

Illinois' 13th District had an illustrious history, having
been the site of civil rights and good-government battles
that resonated across the country. It spanned Hyde Park
mansions, South Shore bungalows and poverty-bitten
precincts in Englewood. It was in this part of the city
that an eager reform Democrat named Abner Mikva had
first entered political office in the 1950s; he would later
become a congressman, judge and White House counsel.
And here a young, brash minister named Jesse Jackson
had run Operation Breadbasket, leading marchers who
sought to pressure grocery chains to hire minorities.

Obama was initially cautious about jumping into the
race. He asked Palmer whether she was sure that she
didn't want to file for re-election to the state Senate as
a fallback, in case her congressional bid failed. Once he
publicly announced his candidacy, Obama told Palmer, he

would throw himself into fundraising, open an office, hire staff and start building support, and it would be hard for him to withdraw. Palmer assured him she had no intention of running for her old seat.

So in July 1995, Barack Obama launched his first race for political office. As fall faded into a cold Chicago winter, he emerged as a gifted campaigner who, after finishing hectic workdays, would layer on thermal underwear to knock on South Side doors. In impromptu street-corner conversations and media interviews, he disparaged local pols for putting self-preservation ahead of public service. At the last house on a dark block, "he would start a discussion that should have taken five minutes, and pretty soon someone was cooking him dinner," recalled Carol Anne Harwell, a consultant to his campaign.

Obama ran on a reformist message, but from the beginning he showed an affinity for the basics of old-fashioned politicking. Chief among these were raising money and attracting powerful allies. Those skills came together in the person of Antoin "Tony" Rezko, an astute navigator of the city's political byways who would later be convicted on federal corruption charges and become a major embarrassment for Obama. Born in 1955 in Aleppo, Syria, to a Christian family in a Muslim area, Rezko settled in Chicago and gravitated toward real estate, at first buying vacant South Side parcels and building modest single-family homes. He also invited a growing network of friends to invest in a variety of fast-food restaurants, starting with a chain of Panda Express Chinese eateries.

As his fortune grew, Rezko carefully cultivated well-placed Chicago politicians, such as aldermen who controlled important zoning and land-use decisions, and he was always on the lookout for up-and-coming politicians to court. Rezko first reached out to Obama around 1990, when the young Chicagoan was making headlines as the first African-American president of the Harvard Law Review. Rezko and two of his real estate partners called out of the blue to offer Obama a job building inner-city homes. Obama said no, but the two remained on friendly terms. And when Obama announced his candidacy for state Senate, his earliest seed money came from Rezko. In July 1995, the campaign's first month, Obama received $2,000 from Rezko-controlled companies.

Obama also proved skilled at winning over the press. A highly laudatory article in the Chicago Reader, a respected alternative newspaper, depicted Obama as a brilliant visionary, almost a prophet. "He wants to stand politics on its head, empowering citizens by bringing together the churches and businesses and banks, scornful

grandmothers and angry young," the article said. "Mostly he's running to fill a political and moral vacuum." Given the nature of the district, Obama in his first race ran much more as a representative of the black community than he would in his later campaigns for U.S. Senate and for president. But much of his language and message, on forming grand alliances to achieve practical solutions, would remain remarkably consistent.

The campaign moved along smoothly, especially given that it was Obama's first foray into politics. Then Palmer's congressional bid collapsed. On Nov. 28, 1995, she placed a distant third in the race to replace Reynolds. The winner was Jesse Jackson Jr., son of the famous civil rights activist, who successfully portrayed himself as an exciting newcomer and heir to a legendary name. Having lost, Palmer, despite saying she wouldn't run, now reconsidered her decision to give up her state Senate seat. She announced that, due to an "outpouring" of support, she was switching gears and running for her old position after all. "Michael Jordan can come back, and so have I," Palmer declared. Obama was furious. He liked and admired Palmer, and had been grateful for her backing. But now, in public comments, he framed her reversal in moral terms, saying it was "indicative of a political culture where self-preservation comes in rather than service." He added, "I am disappointed that she's decided to go back on her word to me."

Palmer had built up a lot of support over the years, and some of her allies tried to persuade Obama to step aside and let her retake her seat. An anguished Obama tried to decide what to do. He sought advice from political veterans, and they urged him to hold his course. "I thought the world of Alice Palmer," said one, state Rep. Barbara Flynn Currie, but "at that point she had pulled her own plug." Obama ultimately agreed. He decided to hold firm and defy Palmer, but it was not an easy choice. "I really saw turmoil in his face," Harwell said.

Palmer's supporters then invited Obama to the home of a local state representative for talks, in a last-ditch attempt to get him to change his mind. But by then his mind was made up. Obama arrived alone, and the session did not last long. "It was a brief meeting," recalled Timuel Black, a Palmer friend who also knew Obama. "He did not put it in inflammatory terms, he just did not back away. It was not arguments, it was stubbornness. Barack had by then gone ahead in putting together his own campaign, and he just didn't want to stop."

Then Obama took one more step. It was one thing to stick to his decision to run for state Senate. Now he proceeded to push Palmer out of the race entirely. To get on the ballot, Palmer needed to file nominating petitions signed by at least 757 district voters, and she had only a few days to do so. Just in time for the filing deadline on Dec. 18, 1995, Palmer submitted 1,580 signatures, about twice the required number. But Obama's campaign operatives realized that Palmer had had to gather the signatures hastily, and they decided to scrutinize them to make sure they were legitimate. Ronald Davis, an Obama consultant whom Obama called his "guru of petitions," and Alan Dobry, a Democratic activist, began poring through Palmer's nominating petitions.

It didn't take long for them to see that hundreds of the names did not represent legitimate voters in the district.

Obama entered the Illinois state Senate in 1997.

"We looked at those petitions and found that none of them met the requirements of the law," Dobry said. "Alice's people, they'd done it in a great hurry. Almost all her petitions were signed a day or so before the deadline." According to Davis, Palmer "had kids gathering the names. I remember two of her circulators, 'Pookie' and 'Squirt.'" Davis urged Obama to file legal challenges to Palmer's petitions, as well as those of three lesser-known Democrats in the race. Such tactics are not uncommon in Chicago; in a recent round of city elections, ballot challenges eliminated 67 of the 245 declared candidates for alderman. Davis told Obama, "If you can get 'em, get 'em. Why give 'em a break? I'm going to knock them all off." Obama asked Davis, "What do you need?" Davis told him, "I need an attorney." Obama asked, "Who is the best?" Davis answered, "Tom Johnson."

Obama already knew Johnson, a civil rights lawyer and fellow Harvard Law graduate who had handled election cases for Mayor Harold Washington and had offered Obama informal legal advice since his activist days. With Johnson's help, Obama's aides were confident. They piled up binders of polling sheets in the election board office on the second floor of City Hall, and on Jan. 2, 1996, they began the tedious process of challenging hundreds of signatures. In time, they showed that Palmer had fewer

than the 757 valid signatures she needed. But Obama's team didn't stop there. The three other Democratic candidates were long shots, but Obama's operatives, not taking any chances, went after them as well. Little-known candidate Marc Ewell had filed 1,286 signatures, but Obama's objections left him 86 short of the minimum, and election officials struck him from the ballot.

Ewell filed a federal lawsuit contesting the election board's decision, but his case was dismissed days later. The judge's decision showed how Ewell was tripped up by complexities in the election procedures, and how Obama in contrast shrewdly understood those complexities and took advantage of them. City authorities had just completed a routine but massive purge of unqualified names that eliminated 15,871 voters from the 13th District rolls. Ewell and other Obama rivals had relied on earlier polling sheets to verify the signatures of registered voters, but Obama's challenges were decided at least in part using the most recent, accurate list.

Another long-shot contender, Gha-is Askia, filed 1,899 signatures, but the Obama team sustained objections to 1,211 of them, leaving him 69 short. Leafing through scrapbooks in his South Shore apartment, Askia, a perennially unsuccessful candidate, acknowledged years later that he had paid Democratic Party precinct workers $5 a sheet for some of the petitions, and he suspected they had used a classic Chicago ruse of passing the papers around among themselves to forge the signatures. "They round-tabled me," Askia said.

Ultimately each of Obama's Democratic rivals was forced out of the race.

CLEARING THE PLAYING FIELD

There are several ways to look at this episode. Undeniably, challenging petition signatures was a legitimate, even commonplace political maneuver, undertaken regularly by Chicago politicians to make sure their rivals were playing by the rules. Yet one of Obama's driving messages, from his earliest activist days through his presidential campaign, has been the importance of expanding access to the ballot box and empowering disenfranchised citizens. In his first bid for office, he used his superior resources and organization to reduce the voters' choices, essentially, to himself. He entered public office not by leveling the playing field, but by clearing it. He claimed his first piece of political power through the rough-and-tumble of Chicago politics.

Askia believed that Obama's actions contradicted his image as a champion of the little guy and a crusader for voter rights. "Why say you're for a new tomorrow, then do old-style Chicago politics to remove legitimate candidates?" Askia said. "He talks about honor and

"There's a legitimate argument to be made that you shouldn't create barriers to people getting on the ballot. [But] to my mind, we were just abiding by the rules that had been set up. If you can win, you should win, and get to work doing the people's business."

Barack Obama

democracy, but what honor is there in getting rid of every other candidate so you can run scot-free? Why not let the people decide?" Obama's move also divided veteran Chicago political activists. "There was friction about the decision he made," said Timuel Black, who had tried to negotiate with Obama on Palmer's behalf. "There were deep disagreements."

Many years later, Obama conceded that "there's a legitimate argument to be made that you shouldn't create barriers to people getting on the ballot." But the tactics were justified, he said, by obvious flaws in his opponents' signature sheets. "To my mind, we were just abiding by the rules that had been set up," he said, adding, "If you can win, you should win, and get to work doing the people's business."

In what has become a common rhetorical device for him, Obama justified his action as not merely good for himself, but for the public. "I gave some thought to … should people be on the ballot even if they didn't meet the requirements," he said. "My conclusion was that if you couldn't run a successful petition drive, then that raised questions in terms of how effective a representative you were going to be." Asked whether the district's primary voters were well-served by having only one candidate, Obama smiled and said, "I think they ended up with a very good state senator."

At the time, however, Obama seemed less at ease with the decision, and he expressed reservations about eliminating his fellow Democrats, if only for appearances' sake. "He wondered if we should knock everybody off the ballot," Davis said. "How would that look?"

Obama did not attend the election board hearings at which his operatives challenged the signatures, though he asked them to call him every night to let him know how it was going. And he did not crow over the tactic's success. "I don't think he thought it was, you know, sporting," said Will Burns, an Obama campaign volunteer who helped with the challenges. "He wasn't very proud of it." Obama also felt discomfort over his personal conflict with Palmer. "I liked Alice Palmer a lot. I thought she was a good public servant," he said. "It was very awkward.

That part of it I wish had played out entirely differently."

As for Palmer, even years later she did not concede the problems that Obama's team found in her signatures. She could have overcome the objections and stayed on the ballot, she insisted, if she'd had more time and resources. It was wrenching to withdraw, she said. "But sit for a moment, catch your breath, get up and keep going," she added. "I'm a very practical person. Politics is not the only vehicle for accomplishing things." Palmer went on to become a special assistant to the president of the University of Illinois.

Obama now had no primary opposition in a heavily Democratic state Senate district, and he coasted to victory against token Republican opposition, becoming the newly minted state senator from the 13th District. In the next dozen years, of course, he was to rocket to the top of the nation's politics with almost unprecedented speed. Since their battle in 1996, Obama said, he and Palmer have not been in touch. "No, not really," he said. "No."

5 "He had other ambitions": In the Illinois legislature

FROM THE MOMENT Barack Obama arrived in the Illinois Senate, it was clear he did not plan to stay. The restless sense of ambition that drove him to jump into the state Senate race was even more apparent now that he held political office. Just a few months into his tenure, Obama approached Mike Hoffman, chief of staff to the state Senate Democrats, and offered to buy him a beer. The two adjourned to a nearby hotel bar, and talk turned to how Obama's unusual name might play in Illinois' conservative downstate areas if he were to seek statewide office. You could actually have fun with a strange name in a campaign, the two men agreed. No specific position came up, like senator or governor, but to Hoffman the freshman's message was clear: "He wanted me to know that he had other ambitions."

Obama went to work furthering those ambitions, quickly cultivating a powerful patron. Emil Jones, leader of the Senate Democrats, the owner of a gravelly voice and tailored suits, was an old-fashioned if pragmatic liberal, a sort of idealistic wheeler-dealer. A former sewer inspector, Jones had worked his way up through state politics, and he liked to quote a saying: "When the elephants fight, the mice get trampled." Then he would add, "Emil's protecting the mice," meaning the state's disadvantaged. To Jones, an older African-American, Obama represented the future, someone who "embodies all that I dream and work for." Jones and Obama had met on a street corner years earlier, when a community group led by Obama had coincidentally convened a meeting near Jones' house, and the two had been close ever since. When Obama arrived in Springfield, Jones took on the task of guiding him through the tricky politics of the capital.

Obama needed such a powerful friend. He had reached office by forcing out a popular member of the Senate's Black Caucus, Alice Palmer, and that hardly endeared him to her former colleagues. Jones may have viewed Obama as a dynamic new leader, but other African-American legislators were put off by the flashy newcomer promising reform, the Harvard-educated lawyer who had been raised in exotic places far from Chicago's West and South Sides. Mindful of such attitudes, Obama, even before taking office, had sought advice from Art Turner, a veteran black state representative from the West Side. Turner warned him not to "come in the door like you're all-knowing," and to "realize that some aren't ready for reform or changes." Obama also reached out to Paul Williams, a lobbyist and longtime political operative, who quickly found himself mediating between Obama and more seasoned black lawmakers. "Let's face it," Williams would say later, "there's certain African-Americans that the world is more likely to fall [for] than others. Barack fits all that stuff: educated, smart, good-looking, lean, all these kinds of things."

Jones soon began handing Obama assignments that would normally have gone to a more senior senator, for example making him the lead Democratic negotiator on a high-profile welfare-to-work package. That did not sit well with longer-serving representatives who felt Obama had not paid his dues. Among the most put out was Sen. Rickey Hendon, a streetwise West Sider nicknamed "Hollywood" who had once hoped to be a movie producer. Another contemptuous colleague was Sen. Donne Trotter, the Democratic point man on budget issues. Hendon and Trotter would "just give Barack hell," disparaging him as a know-it-all, said Sen. Kimberly Lightford, another black colleague.

When Obama presented his first bill on the Senate floor, Hendon rose for some mockery. "Senator, could you correctly pronounce your name for me? I'm having a little trouble with it," he said. He was wondering, Hendon added as laughter filled the chamber, whether Obama might be Irish. "It will be when I run countywide," Obama shot back humorously, referring to the powerful Irish voting bloc in Chicago's Cook County. It was normal for a lawmaker introducing his bill to face some joking questioning as a form of hazing, but Hendon quickly went beyond this to ridicule Obama's bill. At another point Obama and Hendon nearly came to blows. Obama had voted for budget cuts that eliminated a child welfare office in Hendon's district. Hendon, on the Senate floor, said

Obama had "a lot of nerve to talk about being responsible" to those in need, then voting to cut services for the poor. Obama responded that he hadn't realized he was voting for the cuts. "I would appreciate the next time my dear colleague, Sen. Hendon, ask me about a vote before he names me on the floor," he added. Microphones off, the two men headed to the back of the Senate chamber, where Obama tried to put his hand on Hendon's shoulder. Hendon slapped it away. Asked about the incident later, Hendon said, "My memory is foggy on that issue. It's going to remain foggy."

Obama's tense relationship with some key African-American lawmakers was all the more striking given how tightly he bonded with three white colleagues. They became his closest friends in Springfield, poker-playing buddies and sounding boards, even though their backgrounds could not have been more different from his. The dynamic seemed to reflect Obama's lifelong struggle to straddle different worlds. There was blunt-talking Denny Jacobs, from the Quad Cities, and Larry Walsh, whose aw-shucks demeanor belied deft political skills. Obama was friendliest, perhaps, with Terry Link, who was elected to the Senate at the same time as Obama and shared office space with him. "We were just polar opposites," Link said. "He won easy, I had a difficult race. He was Harvard Law, and I was lucky to get out of high school. He was backed by independents, and here I was a party leader." Yet Link found himself helping Obama, coaching the newcomer on how to develop ties to party insiders, labor unions and other old-line Democratic groups.

THE REGULAR-GUY IMAGE
For all his image as a purist, Obama quickly showed a knack for schmoozing. Nowhere was this on better display than at "The Committee Meeting," the code name for Wednesday night poker games attended by about a dozen lawmakers and lobbyists. Obama was a regular, and his stingy betting became a running joke. "You're a socialist with everybody's money but your own," said Republican State Sen. Bill Brady. The game was held in the headquarters of the Illinois Manufacturers' Association, a business lobby usually at odds with liberals like Obama. Handed a cigar and a cocktail on the way in, players might leave a few hundred dollars richer or poorer. It was a way to develop relaxed friendships outside the polarizing debates of the Capitol dome. For Obama, it was also a chance to prove he was a regular guy, which he did quite consciously. "When it turned out that I could sit down and have a beer and watch a game or go out for a round of golf or get a poker game going, I probably confounded some of their expectations," he said.

Obama developed an ability to use his charm and

Previous page
Illinois state Sen. Obama during a session
in the Senate chambers in May 2002 in Springfield.

With wife Michelle and
daughter Malia at his side,
state Sen. Obama
concedes in March 2000
in Chicago as he
lost the race in the
1st Congressional District
against Rep. Bobby Rush.

"The general perception was, 'Here's this new guy coming in and he is acting holier-than-thou.'"

Barack Obama

eloquence to woo opponents. On one occasion, he spoke so passionately in favor of affirmative action that a Republican colleague shelved a resolution aimed at undermining it at public universities. In another floor debate, state Sen. Peter Roskam, a conservative Republican, told his colleagues, "Part of Sen. Obama's ability, and his tremendous way of gathering votes and support, is that he is very persuasive and puts on a terrific presentation. And that's a sincere compliment." Obama, not to be outdone, declared himself "a member of a mutual admiration society with Sen. Roskam." He went on, in a somewhat gushing manner: "He's always terrific, and I know he's got his family here today. He's produced some beautiful children, which clearly shows to me he knows how to choose a spouse. And we were just talking about the fact that we both improved our DNA with our choices of spouses." Then he added wryly, "Having said that, have I said that he's wrong? I love him, but he's wrong."

Springfield was where Obama grew up as a politician. He spent eight years in the state capital, and it was the last time he could operate outside the glare of an almost blinding national scrutiny. Under the cover of this relative obscurity, Obama was a study in complexity, caution and calculation. Democrats were in the minority for all but his final two years in the Statehouse, and Obama tempered his progressive reform agenda with a cold dash of realism, often forging consensus with conservative Republicans when other liberals wanted to crusade.

He could still be impassioned in favor of a cause, as when he fought for a bill in 1999 that would keep track of the thousands of state residents moving off welfare. "It is easy for these folks to drop out of our line of sight," Obama said. "They generally are not represented down here in Springfield. They don't have powerful lobbies. They do not contribute to our political campaigns." Then he described a family he had spotted recently scrounging for aluminum cans. "A man with a shopping cart. Behind him a mother pushing a baby cart. Baby inside. Midnight," Obama recounted. "This was their visible means of support. This is the job that awaited them if they weren't on welfare. We have an obligation to that family."

Jones, the Senate Democratic leader, chose Obama as the Democrats' point man on ethics reform. He pursued the cause with vigor, putting him at odds with some veteran lawmakers. Sen. Trotter felt Obama swooped in "as the knight on the white horse," making it sound as if everyone in Springfield was corrupt except him. "It wasn't appreciated," Trotter said. Obama dryly acknowledged that the ethics bill "was not a favorite of my colleagues." He added, "The general perception was, 'Here's this new guy coming in and he is acting holier-than-thou.'"

The most awkward moment of Obama's legislative tenure came in late 1999, when lawmakers were debating whether to restore a gun-control law that the courts had struck down. Obama voiced his frustration on the Senate floor, noting that he was supposed to be joining his family in Hawaii for Christmas. "I think everybody is aware that no one is more eager to get out of here than me," Obama told his colleagues. "I'm supposed to be on a beach. It's 85 degrees in Honolulu, last I checked." The gun debate stalemated, and Obama flew to Hawaii. But then a compromise was unexpectedly reached, and lawmakers were called back to vote on it. Obama chose to remain in Hawaii. The deal narrowly failed, and Obama was roundly criticized for missing the vote. An unrepentant Obama attributed his absence to a higher obligation, saying his young daughter was ill and he could not leave her. "I cannot sacrifice the health or well-being of my daughter for politics," Obama said. "I had to make a decision based on what I felt was appropriate for my daughter and my wife. ... If the press takes my absence as the reason for the failure of the Safe Neighborhoods bill, then that's how the press is going to report it."

PROTECTING HIS VIABILITY

His cautious approach was perhaps best exemplified by how he dealt with the issue of abortion. To many, abortion is as close to a morally pure question as politicians face. To its opponents, by and large, it's murder, and no compromise is possible, any more than society could tolerate homicide. To those who support abortion rights, it's a question of respecting a woman's dignity, humanity and control over her own body. During Obama's tenure, the Illinois Senate voted 14 times on various abortion restrictions. On half of these, Obama voted "present" rather than yes or no. Obama had always

U.S. Senate candidate Obama meets with members of the Red Hat Society in October 2004 at a Chicago retirement community.

portrayed himself as strongly pro-choice, so his decision to cast a non-committal vote seemed curious. It was hard to read this as anything other than a way to protect his future viability for higher office. Obama, backed by officials from Planned Parenthood, said the "present" votes were part of a concerted strategy to give cover to Democrats who might risk defeat if they voted "no." But other Democrats do not recall such a strategy, and in any case Obama was hardly in jeopardy of losing a re-election battle in his liberal district.

It is true that voting "present"—Illinois was one of only a handful of states that allowed such votes—was sometimes part of a broader plan. Democrats, when in the minority, would occasionally vote "present" en masse to protest some Republican tactic. On one frenetic day in March 1999, the state Senate considered more than 175 pieces of legislation, with Obama voting "present" on 31 of them. But on almost all those votes, more than a dozen

of Obama's Democratic colleagues also voted "present," as an orchestrated protest against a Republican budget package.

During his time in Springfield, Obama was always looking for the next chance to advance to a bigger stage. At one point this prompted him to make an uncharacteristically reckless and ill-conceived move. Just two years after he took office, word began circulating that Obama would challenge Congressman Bobby Rush. An intriguing figure, Rush was a former Black Panther who had won a seat in Congress in 1992. Ever since, he had walked a delicate line, staying in touch with his Black

Following page
Campaigning for the U.S. Senate, state Sen. Obama addresses University of Illinois students in November 2004.

Power roots while steadily increasing his clout in Congress. The Rush-Obama race in 2000 immediately took on the feel of a generational fight. Rush was a quintessential representative of 1960s black activism, while Obama embodied a new generation. It was not the last time Obama would find himself—or cast himself—in this role of new black leader, later being at odds with such civil rights legends as John Lewis and Jesse Jackson. Rush had deep roots and wide networks in the district, and despite Obama's energetic reform campaign he lost badly. On election night, Rush praised Obama and another opponent, Trotter, as "diamonds indeed," but he never seemed to forget Obama's challenge.

If Obama was chastened by this defeat, he got over it. His next opportunity, a bigger one, came along unexpectedly four years later.

The U.S. Senate is a place most do not leave voluntarily. Senators are treated like emperors by staffers, lobbyists and other supplicants, and they can become addicted to the chamber's powers and comforts. Senate history is filled with stories of those who stayed on into old age and infirmity, long past the time when they could credibly do their job. In 2003, Sen. Strom Thurmond of South Carolina left the chamber at age 100 after serving almost a half-century. He died a short time later. Sen. Robert Byrd of West Virginia was 85 and had served in the Senate for 44 years, two more than Obama had been alive. Sen. Edward Kennedy of Massachusetts, 70, was a relative newcomer, having served 41 years. But to Obama's great fortune, Illinois' junior senator, Republican Peter Fitzgerald, decided that year to depart the Senate after only one term. Fitzgerald faced a tough re-election battle, and he complained of the time and energy that would be required to run another campaign.

About a year earlier, Obama had approached his mentor, Emil Jones, and told him, "You're a very powerful guy." "I've got the power to do what?" Jones responded. "You could help elect a U.S. senator," Obama said. Jones asked his protege whether he had anyone in mind. "Yeah—me," Obama replied. Obama's ambitions were an open secret in Springfield, but making the leap to the U.S. Senate was a long shot. Obama was unknown even to most voters in Chicago, let alone the rest of the state.

When the race began, Obama was far from the favorite in the Democratic field. That status belonged to Blair Hull, a wealthy financier who aired many ads to pump up his name recognition. But Hull's effort

Democrat Barack Obama (left) and Republican Alan Keyes debate on the radio in October 2004 in Springfield, Ill.

In Chicago, U.S. Sen.-elect Obama, daughter Malia, wife Michelle and daughter Sasha celebrate his victory in November 2004.

collapsed when journalists obtained divorce records in which his ex-wife accused Hull of physical and verbal abuse. Obama still faced state Comptroller Dan Hynes, the son of a Chicago ward boss, who had the support of Chicago's Democratic organization. But on primary day, Obama overwhelmed Hynes 54 percent to 23 percent. This campaign provided the first glimpse of Obama's sweeping multiracial appeal. His initial strategy had been to build a coalition of blacks and liberal whites, a well-worn tactic in Illinois politics. He did win over those groups, but Obama surprised even his own strategists by also amassing broad support from suburban and rural areas.

Having won the Democratic primary, Obama faced a formidable Republican opponent in Jack Ryan, an enormously wealthy former investment banker who had been laying the groundwork for a campaign for years. But Ryan, too, was done in by divorce records, as a court gave journalists access to the records of Ryan's split with Jeri Ryan, an actress who played a sexy alien on one of the Star Trek series. The records revealed that she had accused Ryan of taking her to sex clubs and trying to coerce her into having sex with him in front of strangers. Ryan vigorously denied this, but he was forced to withdraw. Suddenly Obama was left with every politician's fantasy, running for a powerful office with no opposition. A month after Ryan's withdrawal, Obama delivered his dramatic keynote address to the Democratic National Convention, making him a national star and putting the race even further out of reach for the Republicans, if that were possible.

The Illinois Republican Party responded, inexplicably, by recruiting Alan Keyes, a fiery politician from Maryland who had already run twice for president, to take on Obama. Keyes was a controversial, inflammatory figure. It was as though Republicans had decided to field their own high-profile African-American candidate, but the choice was otherwise hard to understand. Keyes predictably set about making incendiary comments, such as declaring that if Jesus could vote in Illinois, he would oppose Obama. "Christ would not vote for Barack Obama, because Barack Obama has voted to behave in a way that it is inconceivable for Christ to have behaved," Keyes said. The reporters present, apparently not taking this pronouncement too seriously, asked whether Jesus would vote for Keyes or for a third-party candidate. Keyes modestly demurred, saying, "People will have to make that judgment for themselves."

It was no surprise, then, that on Nov. 2, 2004, Obama won the U.S. Senate race by 70 percent to 27 percent, the largest Senate win in state history. Keyes, characteristically, refused to concede or accept defeat

throughout the night. By this time, he had become a sufficient embarrassment that most prominent Illinois Republicans skipped his election-night event. In contrast, Obama's victory party at the Hyatt Regency Hotel in downtown Chicago was mobbed. The senator-elect promised to bring tangible improvements to the lives of his constituents. "We will not be measured by the margin of our victory, but we will be measured by whether we are able to deliver concrete improvements to the lives of so many people all across this state," he said. At the end of the speech, Obama repeated a phrase he had begun using in his campaign that would get wider exposure before long: "Yes, we can!" With the victory, Obama became only the third African-American elected to the U.S. Senate since Reconstruction. He was filling a seat held recently by Carol Moseley Braun, who had been the second. A year earlier Obama had been a little-known state lawmaker. Now he was coming to Washington not just as a new senator, but with a superstar status rare in recent political history. The question was what he was going to do with it.

In Springfield, Ill., fellow state senators hug Obama at a party in November 2004 after he won election to the U.S. Senate. Left to right are: Terry Link, Denny Jacobs, Obama, Tony Munoz, Emil Jones and Edward Maloney.

6 *"Finding partners and coalitions": In the U.S. Senate*

THREE MONTHS LATER, newly elected United States Sen. Barack Obama and his top advisers sat down to a four-hour meeting fueled by pepperoni pizza and lofty ambition. The charismatic celebrity-politician had just rocketed from the Illinois legislature to the Senate, and the challenge was to keep the public's adulation despite the limited tools available to a freshman senator. Obama and his advisers, with some hubris, were thinking far ahead. Some called it the "2010-2012-2016" plan: a potential bid for governor or re-election to the Senate in 2010, followed by a campaign for the White House as soon as 2012 or, if that seemed too soon, 2016. The advisers knew Obama had something special, and the trick was not to let it dissipate in the muck of daily

Michelle and Barack Obama outside the U.S. Capitol with their daughters, Malia and Sasha, after he was sworn in Jan. 4, 2005.

politics. The way to get there, they decided, was by carefully building a record that matched the senator's image, perfected in his Senate race and Democratic convention speech: Obama as unifier and consensus-builder, as almost post-political leader.

Participants in that after-hours session in February 2005, including adviser David Axelrod, agreed on a low-profile strategy that would emphasize workhorse results over headlines. Obama would invest in his long-term profile precisely by not seeming too eager for the bright lights. The plan mimicked that of the most recent outsize figure to come to the Senate, former First Lady Hillary Clinton. Like Clinton, Obama concluded that the folkways of the Senate, with the unalterable rules of seniority and collegiality, made it impossible to accomplish anything if he came on too strong. At the same time, the team was determined not to follow the path of Carol Moseley Braun, who had come to the Senate in 1993 as a star—the only black woman senator in history—and proceeded to ignore Illinois, become enmeshed in scandal and lose the next election. "My profile outstripped my power in the Senate," Obama said. "I was mindful of the importance of establishing good relationships with my colleagues early on and making sure that people didn't think I bought into all the hype."

As he had in the Illinois Senate, Obama pursued a path of caution and calculation. His campaign speeches may have been filled with the electric language of sweeping change, but his actions were those of a believer in compromise, collegiality and not rocking the boat. By the time Obama walked in the doors of the U.S. Capitol, much of the public had become mesmerized by him, and reporters followed his every move. The pressure was great to balance these near-messianic expectations with the circumscribed pathways of the U.S. Senate. Before he was even sworn in, he was on the cover of Newsweek as the Democrat to watch in 2005, and he and his wife, Michelle, appeared in a spread in Vanity Fair. But the reality was he ranked 99th out of 100 in Senate seniority. Obama joked that this meant he had to sharpen pencils and clean latrines. So the plan called for Obama to turn away from the cameras when he might otherwise have been a resonant voice, an approach likely to disappoint some followers. The new senator chafed at having to

follow Democratic talking points and attend press conferences where he felt like a prop.

Still, he resolved to fit in as best he could, a decision reflected in his choice for chief of staff—Peter Rouse, a Senate insider who had been the top aide to departing Democratic leader Tom Daschle of South Dakota. Obama now would be scheduled on trips that traversed two-lane country roads throughout Illinois. He would do his duty raising money for fellow Democratic senators during the "Power Hour," a regular telephone fundraising commitment set up by party leaders. He would sit through lengthy committee hearings, patiently waiting his last-place turn as the most junior member to ask a question. But first and foremost, Obama, as he had in the state legislature, put a premium on paying homage to Senate elders and forming alliances with political adversaries. "So much of what happens around here depends on relationships and on a committee chairman's willingness to help you out," said Chris Lu, Obama's legislative director. "It helps if those relationships are strong." When asked to speak in 2006 at the Gridiron Dinner—a white-tie-and-tails gathering that brings together Washington's political and media elites—Obama reached for humor to show a bit of humility and deflate expectations. "Most of all," he told reporters gathered for the function, "I want to thank you for all the generous advance coverage you've given me in anticipation of a successful career. When I actually do something, we'll let you know."

Obama's determination to show deference extended even to switching his own vote on the Senate floor. On one occasion, Obama planned to support a measure imposing a ceiling of 30 percent on credit card interest rates and other consumer debt. But when the amendment came up for a vote, Obama was standing near Sen. Paul Sarbanes of Maryland, the senior Democrat on the banking committee, who argued against the measure. "You know, this is probably not a smart amendment for us to vote for," Sarbanes told Obama. "Thirty percent is sort of a random number." So

Ethel Kennedy invited Obama to deliver the keynote address in November 2005 at a ceremony in Washington commemorating the 80th birthday of her husband Robert F. Kennedy.

Previous page
In his temporary basement office, U.S. Sen. Obama meets with staff on Jan. 5, 2005, the day after he was sworn in. The windowless office was used for a few months before his permanent one was ready in the Hart Senate Office Building.

Following page
Freshman Sen. Obama talks about ethics reform on Capitol Hill in November 2005. From left: Hillary Clinton, Patty Murray, Mark Dayton, Barbara Boxer, Dick Durbin, Debbie Stabenow, Harry Reid, Jim Jeffords, Chris Dodd and Carl Levin

Obama joined Sarbanes in voting against it.

Obama received many requests for interviews from TV networks and other media organizations that first year, but he turned down just about every one. Instead, he focused on Illinois. By fall 2005 he had held 39 town hall meetings, the vast majority in small communities outside Chicago. The only national speaking invitations he accepted came from the NAACP and from Rep. John Lewis of Georgia, a civil rights icon. Among his multiple balancing acts was embracing his status as an African-American leader without letting it define him. "We have a certain script in our politics, and one of the scripts for black politicians is that for them to be authentically black they have to somehow offend white people," Obama said. "And then if he puts a multiracial coalition together, he must somehow be compromising the efforts of the African-American community." He added, "To use a street term, we flipped the script."

He sat through many committee hearings from beginning to end, which senators rarely do. Not infrequently, by the end of a committee session, the only two senators left in the room would be the chairman, in his high seat in the center of the dais, and Obama, occupying the lonely seat of a junior senator at the end of the platform. "My job was to work and learn the institution," Obama said. "I'm somebody who generally thinks that listening and learning before you start talking is a pretty good strategy. It's like any other social setting—a new job, a new school, a new town. People appreciate it if you spend a little time getting to know them before you announce that you are looking for attention."

"THE NOVICE AND PUPIL"
One colleague who took note was the powerful chairman of the Senate Foreign Relations Committee, Republican Richard Lugar of Indiana, who invited Obama on a trip through the former Soviet Union to inspect the dismantling of Cold War weapons. Obama meekly played the role of Lugar's disciple. "I very much feel like the novice and pupil," he said on the trip. Upon being told that Lenin had several lovers, he said, "I didn't know Lenin was a player," grinning broadly at his own quip. Obama and Lugar ultimately worked together to pass legislation to control the spread of weapons. "I like him, and I appreciate working with him," said Lugar, a foreign policy expert respected by members of both parties.

Obama heads up the Senate steps to vote
on a bill in November 2005.

"It seems to me that he was adept in finding partners and coalitions and actually was able to achieve results." The partnership with Lugar gave Obama credibility as a politician able to work with leaders of the other party. A former presidential candidate who had seen many fellow senators launch White House bids during his 30-year Senate career, Lugar offered unusually strong praise for Obama. "He does have a sense of idealism and principled leadership, a vision of the future," Lugar said. "At certain points in history, certain people are the ones that are most likely to have the vision or imagination or be able to identify talent and to manage other people's ideas. And I think he does this well."

Within his own party, Obama soon became the spokesman on ethics reform, an extension of the tricky role he had assumed in the Illinois legislature. A reform package that included many of the provisions he championed eventually passed the Senate. But for all these modest achievements, some supporters were disappointed that this soaring speaker had grown so quiet once he took national office. Obama the candidate had spoken out forcefully against the Iraq War, for example, but once he came to Washington he was not a moving force on Iraq, leaving that to colleagues like Sen. Russell Feingold of Wisconsin and Rep. John Murtha of Pennsylvania. They and others spoke out forcefully before Obama gave his first major policy speech on the war, almost 11 months after he took office. Obama during this period wrestled with how to proceed, concerned about the worsening news from Iraq and convinced that the public's mood was turning against the war. But in keeping with the pattern of his political career, he moved cautiously. In the summer of 2005 he considered proposing a plan to partition Iraq, but he backed off the idea when advisers raised two concerns: The proposal was fraught with complexities, and he could be seen as overstepping his expertise. Ultimately Obama delivered a more modest speech in November 2005, five days after Murtha's call for a troop withdrawal, urging a reduction in U.S. troop strength but not a timetable for withdrawal. In a Senate debate the following June, Obama went so far as to vote against an amendment proposed by Feingold and Sen. John Kerry to set a timetable for pulling out of Iraq. Only after Obama announced his presidential exploratory committee did he introduce legislation setting a date for the withdrawal of U.S. combat troops. By then the high-profile bipartisan Iraq Study Group also had endorsed such a deadline, and the move was a safer one.

Obama defended his initial reluctance to call for a troop withdrawal. "At the time, my view was that the [Iraqi] government was still forming, and it would be

important to not give the impression, prior to the formation of that government, that we were already on the way out," Obama said. "Now, what changed? We have the breaking out of a complete civil war, at least a significant low-grade civil war." Some were skeptical of this explanation, including those who took political risks to oppose the war more forcefully. Feingold offered Obama mixed reviews for his handling of Iraq. "I've been pleased that his opposition has intensified over time," Feingold said, but "I was not that happy with his initial opposition to a timeline." Still, Feingold credited Obama with taking a stronger stand than other potential presidential candidates. "Of all the people I've worked with that are running for president, I think Sen. Obama probably made the proposal that was most helpful in moving the [Senate Democratic] caucus in the direction I would like to see it go," Feingold said.

Obama's path on other issues, such as energy, carried a whiff of parochial politics. He co-sponsored legislation requiring annual improvements in cars' fuel efficiency— but concentrated on promoting alternative fuels, which catered to Illinois industries. Reflecting the interests of southern Illinois coal producers, he sponsored legislation to provide incentives for refineries that turned coal into liquid fuel, generating criticism from environmentalists. Obama said publicly that nuclear power should be part of the solution to global warming—good news for Exelon Corp., the giant nuclear plant operator based in Illinois, whose executives and employees had donated generously to Obama's campaigns.

But for the most part, Obama's voting had a decidedly liberal tilt. He spoke out for increasing the minimum wage, for funding stem cell research and against banning desecration of the flag. He did break with liberals in a few significant instances, voting, for example, to confirm Condoleezza Rice as secretary of state. He voted against both of Bush's choices for the Supreme Court, but sided with conservatives three times on other controversial Bush judicial nominees. Perhaps one of the most surprising breaks with liberal interest groups came early in his term, when Obama voted for a bill to give federal courts jurisdiction in more class-action lawsuits.

In all, the result was modest legislative achievement. His friends said that Obama accomplished a good deal given the time and tools at his disposal. But several

Obama confers with Sen. John McCain (R-Ariz.) as others discuss an immigration bill during a news conference in Washington in March 2005. In foreground is Sen. Edward Kennedy; top right is Sen. Joe Lieberman.

Republican senators felt that Obama was not making much of a mark in Washington. "He's easy to get along with. I admire him. I enjoyed reading his book. But he hasn't been here long enough to have an impact on the Senate," said Republican Sen. Lamar Alexander of Tennessee. "It's like asking how's a football player doing halfway into the first quarter. It's too early to say." Sen. Trent Lott of Mississippi added, "I don't think he has enough experience to be president of the United States, particularly in defense and foreign policy areas and overall in domestic areas. But overall, in the Senate, he has done a good job."

For all his careful planning, during his first year in the U.S. Senate Obama made one of the most foolish moves of his career, an action he would later call "boneheaded." Perhaps his rapid rise had whetted Obama's appetite for a nice house; he would hardly be the first politician with such a desire. The Obamas' income, bolstered by two best-selling books, was $1.67 million at this point. Obama had come from a modest background and had never shown a particular interest in money. After graduating from Harvard Law School, he could have commanded an enormous salary at a major law firm, but instead chose a path focused on activism, academia and politics.

But in 2005, not long after Obama came to Washington, he and his wife, Michelle, decided to buy a stately $1.65 million house on Chicago's South Side. The 96-year-old Georgian Revival home had four fireplaces, bookcases fashioned from Honduran mahogany and a 1,000-bottle wine cellar, quite a contrast with the modest house in Jakarta where Obama had lived as a child. The problem came with the involvement of Antoin "Tony" Rezko. A real estate developer and businessman who had made a practice of cultivating rising stars in Chicago politics, Rezko was on friendly terms with Obama and had made generous contributions to his political campaigns. At the time Obama was buying his house, however, it was being reported that Rezko was under federal grand jury scrutiny, which should have made Obama wary. But Obama took Rezko on a tour of his prospective new home, and on the day the Obamas bought the house, Rezko and his wife bought the adjoining vacant lot for $625,000. The Obamas wanted a fence between the two parcels, and Rezko agreed to build and pay for the $14,000 wrought-iron fence. Obama also wanted some space between his house and the fence, so Rezko agreed to sell him 10 feet of property.

In all, it looked very much like Obama, an up-and-coming politician, was accepting favors from an ethically challenged operator. Obama denied this was true, saying he had not violated any ethical rules and had been careful to pay Rezko above the appraised value for the strip of property. He had never worked with Rezko on any legislative or other government matters, he added. But after the transaction was detailed in the Chicago Tribune, Obama was remorseful, saying he realized he had made an error. His dealings with Rezko were ethical, he said, but he now understood how bad they looked. "It was a mistake to have been engaged with him at all in this or any other personal business dealing that would allow him, or anyone else, to believe that he had done me a favor," Obama said in a written statement. "For that reason, I consider this a mistake on my part and I regret it."

A RISING PROFILE

As his second year in the Senate rolled around, Obama carefully began to make greater use of the bully pulpit at his disposal. He dotted his 2006 calendar with a few high-profile speeches, including one on energy policy and a well-received address on the role of faith in politics. He used his second book, "The Audacity of Hope," to promote his policy ideas. Staffers spent nights and weekends scouring the chapters as they rolled in, looking for potential political pitfalls—a vetting committee Obama lacked when he published his earlier, more provocative memoir. When Obama wanted to name someone as the epitome of left-leaning politics, an aide urged him to use a House member instead of a Senate colleague. So the book cites future Speaker Nancy Pelosi of California as a quintessential liberal, even though Obama's voting record is similar to hers. And through it all the public fascination with Obama continued, despite the lack of soaring addresses or dramatic achievements. The media chronicled his summer pilgrimage to Africa, a poignant part of his personal story, as though it were a presidential visit.

A crucial development was the success of Obama's campaign appearances for Democrats in the 2006 congressional elections, when the party captured both houses of Congress. Wherever he went, it seemed, crowds turned out. Obama's celebrity also gave him entree to some of the nation's wealthiest and best-connected people, and he put that access at the disposal of his fellow Democrats. Obama was one of the first to call Pelosi on election night and congratulate her on becoming the presumptive speaker of the House. Given the response Obama was receiving as he campaigned for others, his friend and strategist David Axelrod realized Obama would have to at least think about running for president much sooner than planned. "But it wasn't at all clear where that conversation would go," Axelrod said. "If you're going to consider this, we'd better get together and run through what it would entail—whether it's doable, whether it's advisable and, ultimately, whether you feel like you want to do it."

Sen. Ken Salazar (D-Colo.) chats with Obama on the Senate subway as they head to Capitol Hill for a vote in November 2005. The two were ranked at the bottom in Senate seniority.

Obama marveled even more at the success of his book. When he first came to the Senate, many thought his star quality might fade. But his reception on the book tour, as on the congressional campaign circuit, suggested voters' enthusiasm for him was not so ephemeral. With popular opinion turning against the Iraq War, many of Obama's friends thought his time to run for president was not in 2012 or 2016, as in the original plan, but now. One of these was Illinois' senior senator, Democrat Dick Durbin. "These opportunities come around once, at best twice in a lifetime," Durbin told Obama. "You ought to think about that seriously."

And he did. Obama articulated his thoughts in a discussion with the Chicago Tribune's editorial board about a possible presidential run. "First of all, it requires some megalomania. It's kind of crazy," he acknowledged. But he could not avoid a feeling that he might have lucked into being the right person at the right time. "What I at least think about is—whether through luck or happenstance or serendipity or convergences between my biography and events—do I have a particular ability to bring the country together around a pragmatic, common-sense agenda for change that probably has a generational element to it as well?" He recognized that he had little national experience but thought the public's disenchantment with the Iraq War might leave an opening for a candidate to argue that what mattered was not experience but judgment. "The test of leadership in my mind is not going to be what's on a paper résumé," Obama said. "Dick Cheney and Donald Rumsfeld had the best résumé on paper of any foreign policy team, and the result has been what I consider to be one of the biggest foreign policy mistakes in our history." And he speculated on the kind of campaign the Republicans might run, especially if John McCain was their nominee. "Look, if it's John McCain, then [it's going to be] 'war hero against snot-nosed rookie,'" Obama said, more than two years before the parties' 2008 nominees were selected. "I don't think you need a lot of imagination to figure out how they would run that campaign: 'We live in dangerous times. Terrorism's looming. We need a battle-tested leader, and that's John McCain.' I think that's how they present it."

The morning after the November congressional election, with Democrats exulting in their recapture of the House and Senate, a group of Obama friends and advisers met once again, this time at Axelrod's office in Chicago. Obama was ready to talk. Seated around the table in the conference room, the political veterans spoke in unvarnished terms. They gave Obama a primer on running a presidential campaign, emphasizing the relentless organizational and personal demands. They carefully examined the question of how—and whether—they could even put together such a campaign so quickly. When the meeting broke up, the people who had carefully mapped Obama's cautious Senate career had a new task to consider: an audacious, caution-be-damned run for the presidency in 2008.

Previous page
Obama (left) and Republican Sen. Richard Lugar of Indiana
(center) arrive in Azerbaijan in August 2005 on a trip through
the former Soviet Union to inspect the dismantling of
Cold War weapons.

Obama says goodbye to Ukrainian President Viktor
Yushchenko after their meeting in Kiev in August 2005 as part
of the senator's trip with Richard Lugar (foreground).

Following pages
Obama walks onto a makeshift stage to address a large crowd
outside a school in his family's village of Kogelo, Kenya,
in August 2006.

Kenyans in Kisumu wait for Obama's arrival.

7 *"Our souls are broken": Michelle Obama*

IT BECAME INCREASINGLY obvious in early 2007 to those following politics that Obama would run for president, and as a result another figure began attracting significant notice: His wife, Michelle. Just as the senator was the subject of public fascination, many voters were intrigued by the accomplished black woman who could become first lady. In February, Ebony magazine published a cover photo of the Obamas under the headline, "America's next first couple." Other magazines followed suit in coming months. Newsweek put Michelle on its cover, and inside a writer opined, "She is a strong, smart black woman who does not hesitate to speak her mind—and that has been the source of her appeal." Us Weekly magazine took a break from its stories on entertainers like Angelina Jolie and Jessica Simpson to feature an article portraying Michelle as an everywoman. "Michelle Obama: Why Barack Loves Her," the cover read. "She shops at Target, loved 'Sex and the City' and never misses the girls' recitals." The issue was a big seller. On top of that, Michelle's fashion sense, including tailored suits and strings of pearls, attracted the notice of designers and prompted comparisons to Jacqueline Kennedy.

Obama's message had been infused with Michelle's sensibilities for years. One example was a Father's Day sermon Obama delivered in 2005 at Christ Universal Temple, an African-American church in Chicago, aimed squarely at the black community. "There are a lot of folks—a lot of brothers—walking around, and they look like men. They've got whiskers, they might even have sired a child," Obama had said, prompting laughter. "But it's not clear to me that they are full-grown men. What I mean by that is, one of the difficulties that African-American men in particular face is that many of us grew up without fathers." He went on to urge black men to be better parents and take an active role in their children's lives. In another black church, on another Father's Day a few years later, Obama told the congregation, "Any fool can have a child. That doesn't make you a father. It's the courage to raise a child that makes you a father." This was classic Obama, seeking to transcend an old divide in which blacks blamed racism for their problems and whites blamed blacks for their attitudes. But the words also reflected Michelle's outlook to a significant degree. "There's a big part of his message that is about personal responsibility," said Dan Shomon, who was a top Obama adviser for many years. "It's that you can't teach kids to learn if the TV's on. You've got to turn the TV off and take personal responsibility, not just at home but in the community and in the world. That comes from Michelle."

Michelle Obama's Princeton University graduation photo.

In Obama's telling, he was drawn to Michelle Robinson from the moment they met, when he was a summer associate at the Chicago law firm Sidley Austin and she was his mentor. Michelle Robinson was reluctant to date Obama at first, because going out with your protege hardly seemed professional and because it might appear "tacky," as she put it, to date the only other black person in the office. But Obama persisted even after she tried to set him up with other women. Ultimately Michelle relented, and on their first date they got ice cream at Baskin-Robbins. "I asked if I could kiss her," Obama recounted in "The Audacity of Hope." "It tasted of chocolate." Michelle was an intelligent, attractive woman who, like Obama, had attended Harvard Law School and was drawn to politics. As Obama got to know her family, its solidity

Previous page
Michelle Obama is introduced at a Des Moines rally in December 2007, where she appeared with her husband, Barack, and with talk show host Oprah Winfrey.

appealed to him, so different from his own rootless childhood of moving from one country to another without a father. Michelle's home life reminded him of "Leave It to Beaver." Her father suffered from multiple sclerosis but went to work every day at the Chicago water department and attended all his children's extracurricular activities. Michelle's mother was a patient tutor, always available for her son and daughter. "We learned from the best how a happy home should operate," said Michelle's brother, Craig Robinson. "Michelle has very high expectations based on that."

It did not take long for Barack and Michelle's relationship to become entwined with Chicago politics. In the summer of 1991, Valerie Jarrett, deputy chief of staff to Mayor Richard Daley, offered Michelle a job. Michelle called back a day later, saying not "yes" but "maybe." First, she said, her fiance wanted to meet Jarrett. "My fiance wants to know who is going to be looking out for me and making sure that I thrive," Robinson told Jarrett. It was a bit of a strange request, but Michelle was a highly desirable employee, and Jarrett agreed. So the three of them — the prospective boss, the job applicant and the man she would marry — piled into a booth at a seafood restaurant and got to know each other over a long dinner. At the end of the evening, Jarrett turned to Obama and asked, "Well, did I pass the test?" Obama smiled, put his head down, closed his eyes and said, "Yeah, you passed the test."

FAMILY TENSIONS

After the Obamas married in 1992, it became increasingly clear that merging their respective personal and political lives would not be easy. The pressure increased with Obama's entry into politics and the birth of the couple's two daughters, Malia and Sasha. "When I launched my ill-fated congressional run, Michelle made no pretense at being happy with the decision," Obama recounted in "The Audacity of Hope." "By the time Sasha was born — just as beautiful, and almost as calm as her sister—my wife's anger toward me seemed barely contained. 'You only think about yourself,' she would tell me. 'I never thought I'd have to raise a family alone.'" That tension came to form a strand in Obama's political message, as he talked to audiences about the importance of family, the role of parents and the pressures facing women. It also at times devolved into a shtick, albeit one with the goal of humanizing a candidate who all too often seemed cool and remote. At one campaign luncheon for prominent Chicago women, Michelle Obama said her husband had forgotten to put away the butter that morning. "I'm like, 'You're just asking for it. You know I'm giving a speech about you today,'" she told the crowd in mock exasperation. Of course, she also praised Obama

Barack Obama, with then-fiancé Michelle, in Kibera, a slum in Nairobi, Kenya. It was their first trip to Africa together, in the early 1990s.

and asked for the crowd's financial and political support. But her style was supportive, not deferential. "He's a gifted man," she said. "But in the end, he's just a man." Obama, for his part, made a point of letting audiences know he was not above washing dishes and changing diapers. In another passage from his book, Obama recounted how one night after he became a U.S. senator, he called his wife and began excitedly describing an arms-control bill he had sponsored with Sen. Richard Lugar. Preoccupied with matters closer to home, Michelle interrupted to say they had ants in the house and he should buy ant traps on the way home. "I hung up the receiver," Obama recounted dryly, "wondering if Ted Kennedy or John McCain bought ant traps on the way home from work."

More than a spokeswoman, Michelle had become a crucial part of the Obama package as the presidential run approached, complementing and shaping her husband. She had a practical quality that could seem absent from the candidate, with his lofty talk of "hope" and "change." This could be overstated—Obama had his pragmatic side, and his wife could be idealistic—but Michelle Obama put an emphasis on the practical notion of being able to make one's way in the world that seemed alien to Obama. In an equally intangible way, Michelle's background, rooted in a working-class neighborhood on Chicago's South Side, lent a certain credibility to her husband, who consistently battled questions from some blacks about whether he was "authentically" black. The son of an African man and a white woman, Obama had not descended from slaves, as had most African-Americans, and he did not grow up in a typical urban neighborhood, or even in the continental U.S. Michelle Obama heard such talk many times, and it reminded her of comments aimed at her when she was young. "I heard that growing up—'You talk like a white girl,'" she said. "There isn't one black person who doesn't understand that dynamic."

Michelle and Barack Obama appear at a rally in Evansville, Ind., on the night of the Pennsylvania primary in April 2008.

Overall, Obama's family—an appealing wife and two adorable girls—was an undeniable political asset. It created an implicit contrast with the politicians who were to be his biggest adversaries in the presidential campaign, Hillary Clinton and John McCain. Clinton's husband, former President Bill Clinton, was a well-known womanizer who had infamously had an affair with a White House intern. McCain had divorced his first wife under circumstances that struck some as callous. In contrast, the Obama family looked enviably solid, something especially important, perhaps, for a politician who was young, liberal and African-American. Meanwhile, the role of the political spouse had become more complicated over the years. Bill Clinton, in his first run for president, had offered himself and his wife as "two for the price of one," an idea not to everyone's liking. Women like Laura Bush and Cindy McCain, in contrast, took more traditional paths. There was no question which model the Obamas were following. "She's tough," Obama said of Michelle. "There's something about her that projects such honesty and

strength. It's what makes her such an unbelievable professional, and partner, and mother, and wife." The "partner" approach carried political risks, of course, as evidenced by the vitriol directed at Hillary Clinton after she emerged on the national stage, announcing that she was not the type of woman to stay home and bake cookies.

A big part of Michelle's role in Obama's public life had been to communicate to women that she, and by extension her husband, understood and empathized with their burdens. "With the exception of the campaign trail and life in the public eye, I have to say that my life now is really not that much different from many of yours," she told a largely female audience in early 2007. "I wake up every morning wondering how on Earth I am going to pull off that next minor miracle to get through the day. I know that everybody in this room is going through this. That is the dilemma women face today. Every woman that I know, regardless of race, education, income, background, political affiliation, is struggling to keep her head above water."

But she was a forceful, opinionated person and did not hesitate to announce her own views on a variety of matters. In contrast to her husband's optimistic message, Michelle sometimes offered a lengthy critique of America, dwelling on it before adding that Obama was the cure. That was notably true in a February 2008 speech in Los Angeles that attracted derisive commentary from conservative bloggers. "We are still a nation that is too divided," she told a large rally at UCLA. "We live in isolation, and because of that isolation, we fear one another. We don't know our neighbors, we don't talk, we believe that our pain is our own. We don't realize that the struggles and challenges of all of us are the same. We are too isolated. And we are still a nation that is still too cynical." She added, "Things have gotten progressively worse throughout my lifetime, through Democratic and Republican administrations." And she continued, "Barack Obama is the only person in this race who understands that, that before we can work on the problems, we have to fix our souls. Our souls are broken in this nation. We have lost our way." The bleak portrait of America — and with the messianic suggestion that only Obama could repair Americans' inner lives — sparked predictable contempt in conservative circles. So did Michelle's comment, around the same time, that she was proud of her country for the first time in her adult life, presumably due to Obama's political success.

"IT'S A ROLE MODEL THING"

Behind the scenes, she played a strong role in keeping Obama in line, pressing him hard to stop smoking, for example. She was passionate about this partly because her own parents had smoked, and she had hated it. As children, she and her brother had pulled tobacco out of their parents' cigarettes and doused them with hot sauce. When Michelle agreed to support Obama's presidential bid, she imposed a demand—no cigarettes—and Obama quit days before declaring his candidacy. "To me it's a role model thing," she said. "You can smoke or you can be president." This insistence on personal responsibility was reflected in her husband's views on health care and other issues. "This is how he thinks about the problems that we face," Michelle said. "You can't just talk about improving education without talking about improving pay for teachers or making sure that parents are doing their part. ... People have to change their behavior, in addition to systems and institutions changing."

Michelle's professional career had been an asset for Obama. She had developed a network of friends and associates that gave her husband access to some of the city's elite circles of influence. The young Michelle Robinson, a graduate of Princeton University and Harvard Law School, had not stayed long in her position as a $60,000-a-year mayoral assistant. Within weeks, Daley promoted her boss to run the city's Department of Planning and Development, and Michelle followed. "She had this incredible ability to be a problem-solver," said co-worker Beth White. "She was just totally unflappable." Michelle quickly picked up a reputation for being blunt. Once a junior staffer came to White and Michelle to talk about a promotion. Michelle walked the woman step-by-step through her shortcomings. "It wasn't a put-down," White said. "It was simply 'you're not ready for this, and here's why.' She did it kind, but firm. A lot of people are uncomfortable doing that." Michelle soon left city government to launch the Chicago chapter of Public Allies, a group that arranged apprenticeships for young adults at non-profit organizations. Those who worked for her at Public Allies said she challenged them to step outside their comfort zones, especially those involving class and race. "The most powerful thing she ever taught me was to be constantly aware of my privilege," said Beth Hester, a former staffer. Hester, who is white, said Obama helped her overcome her tendency to avoid difficult situations with people of other races or cultures. "Michelle reminded me that it's too easy to go and sit with your own," Hester said. "She can invite you, in kind of an aggressive way, to be all you can be."

After three years at Public Allies, Michelle was recruited by the University of Chicago, eventually going to work for the school's medical center. For all its national prestige, the hospital had a big problem: It was spending millions to treat neighborhood residents who showed up in its emergency room with ailments that would be better handled at local doctors' offices. The university wanted to stop providing this treatment, but the matter was sensitive from a public relations standpoint. The world-class hospital could not simply tell its low-income, underinsured African-American neighbors to go elsewhere. Michelle Obama was charged with tackling the problem. And in many ways, she was well-positioned to do so. "Because she is of color, that gives her some credibility," said Wendy Cox, chief executive of Chicago Family Health Center, which served low-income minority families. Michelle brought together health-care providers and community leaders. She talked about African-Americans' distrust of the health-care system, about how the lack of insurance kept people from seeking preventive care. Coming from someone else, the message might have seemed provocative or condescending. But Michelle could speak of growing up not far from the hospital herself, and recall how family members waited until they got truly sick and then went to the best ER they could find. "It's the most ineffective way to provide care," she said. "And it's the most expensive."

Her strategy was to help patients build relationships with doctors so they could avoid the problems that sent them to the ER in the first place. She created a screening system in the waiting room — where people had routinely showed up with a lunch and camped out to wait for a doctor — to search for people who didn't belong there. After treating those individuals, hospital employees would sit and talk with them. Michelle Obama's staff would refer them to specific clinic doctors, even schedule appointments. The program did not yield dramatic results immediately, but hospital officials were hopeful. Michelle argued that while the uninsured were victims of the system, they also had an obligation to take care of themselves. "It's mutual responsibility," she said. "Whatever health-care solution we bring to the table, people have to use it. People have to put good food in their bodies. People have to take their medication as directed. People can't sit and completely blame outside forces." It was easy to see how that philosophy was expressed in her husband's rhetoric.

Michelle Obama's career has at times caused problems for her husband, mostly because her income has risen along with his political ascent. A Harvard-trained lawyer, she had opted against private practice, and her salary was no doubt small compared to what she could have commanded at a top law firm. But that did not protect her from criticism. Not long after Obama entered the U.S. Senate, Michelle was offered a position on the board of TreeHouse Foods, a maker of specialty foods that is based in Westchester, Ill. In 2006, the company paid her $51,200 for her board activities. Factoring in stock options and other payments, the value of her compensation package was $101,083, according to a filing with the Securities and Exchange Commission. But TreeHouse packaged foods for retailers, and by far its largest customer was Wal-Mart, a company that has become a symbol for liberals of all that is wrong with corporate America. Obama himself had been sharply critical of Wal-Mart's business and labor practices, attacking the giant retailer for paying low wages and providing poor benefits while making enormous profits. Ultimately Michelle resigned from TreeHouse.

At her main job, at the University of Chicago hospital, she was promoted to vice president for community and external affairs in early 2005, shortly after her husband was sworn in to the U.S. Senate. The promotion more than doubled her hospital salary, which soon surpassed $300,000, raising questions about whether the hospital

Michelle Obama introduces her husband in Concord, N.H., in January 2008.

was seeking her husband's goodwill. Michelle saw such questions as sexist and unfair. "I'm a vice president at an academic medical center," she said. "Barack and I have built a joint life together that consists of having two strong individual people who have built careers. Barack hasn't relied deeply on me for his career path, and I haven't relied on him at all for mine. ... I understand why people want to make sure that somehow I'm not using my husband's influence to build my career. And I haven't." Hospital executives said her promotion was based on her outstanding performance and her salary was in line with that of the medical center's 16 other vice presidents. She also earned about 25 percent less than her counterpart at Northwestern Memorial Hospital. "My concern was that somebody was going to recruit her," said Michael Riordan, then president of University of Chicago hospitals.

This was the woman who, if Obama won, would replace Laura Bush at the White House. Just as Americans were confronted with the prospect of a black man in the Oval Office for the first time, they were also contemplating the notion of a black woman filling the role of first lady. With a few exceptions, the president's wife in recent years had possessed a certain prim, bland public personality, from Lady Bird Johnson to Nancy Reagan to Laura Bush. The first lady stood supportively, often adoringly, at her husband's side, taking on worthwhile causes like mental illness or literacy but, while inevitably described as the president's "closest adviser," staying far from policy matters. Many voters were still uneasy at the idea of a president's wife who was forceful and engaged, partly because of an ongoing sexism and conventionality and partly, perhaps, because of a reasonable proposition that, after all, they had not elected the spouse. Hillary Clinton's foray into health care as first lady had been a disaster. Other than Clinton, no first lady had pursued a high-powered professional career as her husband had risen in the political world. And, of course, the first lady had always been white. Michelle Obama—an outspoken, professionally accomplished African-American woman from the South Side of Chicago—is as different from the traditional first lady as her husband is from the mold of previous presidents. As a proliferation of pro-Michelle groups and Web sites suggested, that was exciting for many, and no doubt less so for others. In any case, it was yet another thing for voters, already dazzled by the new-ness of the Obama phenomenon, to contemplate.

Campaigning without her husband, Michelle Obama walks onto the stage before speaking in York, Pa., in April 2008.

8 *"Endless possibility": Running for president*

IT WAS THE KIND of affectionate gesture common among married couples. Michelle Obama gave her husband a last-minute look-over and brushed a few specks of lint from his wool coat. They were waiting in a vestibule of Illinois' Old State Capitol building, the site of the famous "house divided" speech Abraham Lincoln delivered two years before he was elected president. The candidate leaned down to hug his daughters. First Malia, the elder, then Sasha, the younger. He got a kiss from his wife. Then he stood silently and closed his eyes for a few moments, as if lost in thought or, perhaps, a prayer. It was time. The charismatic senator and his young, photogenic

With daughters Malia (left) and Sasha at their side, Michelle Obama brushes lint off Barack's coat in Springfield, Ill., just before the senator declared he was running for president on Feb. 10, 2007. Rev. Jeremiah Wright, pastor of Trinity United Church of Christ, who would later become a controversial figure, is behind Michelle and Barack.

family walked out onto a wooden platform and onto the nation's television screens. From now on, there would be few private moments, as the conflicted young man from Hawaii was fully transformed into the most public of figures, defined by his campaign and his political identity. The sky was a clear blue and the sun shone brightly. The Greek Revival Capitol provided a majestic setting, with its limestone columns and red cupola. And the symbolism was inescapable, especially because this was Feb. 10, 2007, two days before Lincoln's birthday. The man who hoped to become the nation's first African-American president had chosen as his starting point a place that summoned the spirit of the Great Emancipator, a young politician who, like Obama, had had little national experience, but who nonetheless emerged from the wilderness to free the slaves, lead the nation through the Civil War, preserve the Union and, along the way, redefine the meaning of American democracy. Obama's chosen site to launch his candidacy was an attempt to link his campaign with the long struggle for freedom in America and the legacy of a man who overcame doubters to become one of the country's greatest presidents.

Even for central Illinois, a region of brutal winters, it was a bitterly cold day, with temperatures in the single digits. And yet people began arriving in the square in front of the Capitol building at 5 a.m., bundled in hats and gloves and stamping their feet to warm themselves. By the time Obama came onstage about 10 a.m., more than 10,000 people filled the square and spilled down the surrounding streets. A group of students from Harvard Law School, Obama's alma mater, had driven 18 hours to be there. Christopher Schnell, a tall, lithe Lincoln historian, brought his 2-year-old son, Adam. He wanted the boy to be a part of history. Obama's 20-minute announcement speech, which he delivered hatless and without gloves despite the cold, established a tone and themes that would remain remarkably consistent

Barack and Michelle Obama, after he announced his candidacy at the Old State Capitol in Springfield, Ill., on Feb. 10, 2007.

Following page
South Carolina Rep. James Clyburn (fourth from left) joins Democratic contenders for president before a debate in Orangeburg, S.C., in April 2007. From left: Sen. Obama, Sen. Chris Dodd, former Sen. John Edwards, Clyburn, Rep. Dennis Kucinich, Sen. Joe Biden, New Mexico Gov. Bill Richardson and Sen. Hillary Clinton. Former Sen. Mike Gravel also participated in the debate

through his campaign. His manner was easy and confident, his outlook optimistic, envisioning "a future of endless possibility stretching before us." He framed his candidacy as a vehicle for generational change, a call to overcome a cynical system crippled by what he described as "the smallness of our politics." Obama also tied his campaign to the rising fervor against the war in Iraq, reminding his audience that he alone among the major presidential candidates had opposed the war from the start. "America, it's time to start bringing our troops home," he said. "It's time to admit that no amount of American lives can resolve the political disagreement that lies at the heart of someone else's civil war." But even as he tapped the powerful passions aroused by the war, he avoided making it a central theme. Instead, he presented his campaign in the broadest terms, brushing by concrete policies and instead concentrating on transcendent ideals, gauzy emotion and poetic abstraction.

CAMPAIGN ABOUT HOPE, NOT RACE

He did not mention the most obvious and exceptional fact about himself as a presidential candidate, one responsible for much of the excitement surrounding him and a reason that 523 credentialed journalists had traveled to Springfield that day: He was a black man. The allusions were there in his speech, but they were safe, connecting Obama with transformative figures of American history. He quoted Martin Luther King Jr., who while controversial in his time now had a place so secure in the American pantheon that he had his own national holiday. The imagery—a call to generational change, a youthful candidate hatless on a cold day, a slim, elegant wife and small children—evoked John F. Kennedy, who broke barriers of intolerance as the first Catholic president. And, of course, there were numerous references to Lincoln, whom Obama described as "a tall, gangly, self-made Springfield lawyer," in case anyone missed the parallels.

Obama closed with the words Lincoln used at Gettysburg to give larger purpose to the Civil War, calling on the nation to join him in ushering in "a new birth of freedom." At its core, Obama's candidacy would be an aspirational candidacy: It would be about hope. But he would take great care that it not be defined narrowly, in terms of the hopes of black people or the civil rights struggle. His campaign above all would be

Michelle Obama and her two daughters, Malia (lower left) and Sasha, talk behind the stage at Iowa State University in Ames as Sen. Obama speaks at a campaign event in February 2007.

about America's hopes. At a time of terrorism and economic unease, an unpopular war and vindictive partisanship, Obama offered his candidacy as an opportunity to reaffirm America's identity as a country of high ideals and infinite possibilities, and in so doing disprove the skeptics, at home and abroad.

At the announcement, Obama called his campaign "an improbable quest." And so it seemed to those watching that day. His immediate opponent was one of the most formidable figures in American politics: Hillary Clinton, a former first lady, a two-term New York senator and a prominent personality for 15 years. Obama may have benefited from celebrity media coverage, but Clinton had been known far better and much longer. She entered the campaign with a powerful network whose origins dated to Bill Clinton's first White House run. Above all, she had the legacy of the Clinton presidency. Bill Clinton's sex scandal and impeachment may have tarnished his reputation, but he was still beloved by most Democrats and many of the liberal-minded independents likely to vote in the primaries. He had been the only Democratic president since Franklin D. Roosevelt to be elected to two terms. And after George W. Bush's presidency brought a stalemated war in Iraq and stagnant middle-class wages, eight years of peace and prosperity under Bill Clinton looked all the better.

Obama, on the other hand, had obvious liabilities. For all the excitement created by his groundbreaking candidacy, it was unclear how Americans would respond to a black candidate. Even many African-Americans were initially wary, worrying that significant numbers of white Americans would not vote for an African-American. Amid signs that the political climate heavily favored the Democrats, many party loyalists did not want to take a needless risk in an election that otherwise looked close to a sure thing. There was also the matter of experience. Obama had been in the U.S. Senate two years and had never previously held national office, nor had he managed an organization of any size. At a time of war and terrorist threat, steady leadership in the White House seemed especially important. In all, the odds appeared stacked against the senator from Illinois. A Gallup Poll taken on the weekend of his announcement showed that Clinton started the campaign with almost double Obama's support, 40 percent to 21 percent.

Still, the country was in a restless mood and the outcome difficult to foresee. Polls showed deep public

The crowd was a mix of white and black, young and old at a Columbia, S.C., rally for Obama in February 2007.

discontent, with President Bush's approval ratings dropping. The Iraq War was highly unpopular. And nobody spoke of change in quite the way Obama did, nor looked so much the part.

At the very moment Obama was onstage, Joe Rospars, a young, Internet-savvy political operative, sat miles away on an unpacked box in his new apartment. If Obama's soaring speech captured one part of the nascent campaign, Rospars' online maneuverings embodied another. Rospars was excitedly watching two screens. On television, Obama, his new boss, was delivering his announcement speech. On Rospars' laptop, a dashboard of statistics was constantly being updated, measuring visitors to the Obama campaign Web site. Click after click, a trickle became a flood. Not only would thousands visit that day, but within 24 hours a staggering 1,000 would take advantage of a feature allowing them to register the creation of an Obama group in their hometown. "You see 'Idaho for Obama' pop up and you start thinking, 'We might be on to something,'" Rospars said. "You could just see it in the first few hours that something was happening."

The moment marked an important convergence, a politician with transformational potential meeting a technology with its own unprecedented possibilities. The emergence of the Internet into a familiar and comfortable part of most Americans' lives presented a wealth of possibilities for an insurgent politician like Obama. Suddenly, a candidate could rapidly convert excitement among everyday people into money and organization. For decades, campaigns had connected with volunteers mostly through local field offices and reached small-dollar donors through direct mail. Now candidates and supporters could communicate instantly at virtually no cost. Campaigns could use e-mail, Web videos and other new tools to deepen their relationship with supporters and maintain enthusiasm through the peaks and valleys of a long campaign. Obama had to find a way around a Democratic power structure that favored Clinton, and the Internet fit his experience as a community organizer. His campaign aides hired a co-founder of Facebook to help run My.BarackObama.com, their social networking site. They brought on a former journalist to write a blog. And when a CNN producer asked for access to film a documentary on Obama, the campaign instead offered her a job doing it for their own Web site.

EARNING CREDIBILITY

As the campaign began in earnest, Obama drew large, enthusiastic crowds, replicating his performance in the recent congressional elections and book tour. But little in the first few weeks provided any reason to re-evaluate his status as an interesting long-shot. True, by March 31, just seven weeks after he declared his candidacy, Obama raised a stunning $25 million, outperforming Clinton's vaunted fundraising network. That gave the campaign credibility with journalists and other professionals, and suggested it would have the financial resources to compete with Clinton. Yet Obama struggled through the summer and into the fall. Clinton was a commanding presence in televised debates, displaying a detailed grasp of policy and a decisive, confident manner. By contrast, Obama was deferential and prone to missteps. He had trouble responding to questions in brief, punchy sound bites. And he sometimes seemed to be thinking through his answers as he spoke, which on television made him look indecisive. Critics began asking if the junior senator from Illinois was up to the challenge. By early fall, the campaign had made little progress cracking Clinton's lead in national polls. Major fundraisers and donors, who in some cases were being teased for the investments they had made in the Obama campaign by friends who were backing Clinton, urged a change in strategy. October brought a low moment. U.S. Rep. John Lewis, a civil rights hero and an influential black leader who had shown a clear affection for Obama, announced he would endorse Clinton. It was the clearest signal yet that people who wanted to bet on a winner were choosing Clinton.

But beneath the surface, Obama was steadily executing his strategy, using his abundant money to build extensive field organizations in key primary states. In most places, Obama was the first candidate on the ground with organizers, and he generally fielded the largest staff. By mid-October, Obama had opened 31 offices across Iowa, more than any other candidate, establishing local headquarters everywhere from Des Moines to tiny Elkader, population 1,374. The intensive ground operation created a structure Obama could use to leverage the enthusiasm of his supporters. The campaign targeted young people and minority voters, both groups that typically did not turn out in high numbers, even establishing "Barack Stars" chapters at high schools around the state.

The campaign was in some sense an extension of Obama's personal history. He had spent years as a community organizer, and his candidacy was simply a bigger organizing campaign, with himself as the cause. This was an entirely different approach from Clinton's. Recent presidential hopefuls had won their party's nomination by overwhelming their opponents almost immediately. Clinton assumed she would do just that, and spent little time organizing in states with later primaries.

Michelle and Barack Obama appear with Oprah Winfrey at a Des Moines rally in December 2007.

Iowa, the first contest, was crucial to Obama's hopes of denting Clinton's momentum and seizing the advantage. Crucially, a win in Iowa would prove that Obama could prevail in one of the whitest states in the country. Even African-Americans wondered if Obama could win wide support among whites, and the campaign calculated that a win in Iowa would stir a wave of support among African-Americans, helping him win a few weeks later in South Carolina. On a visit to Davenport, Iowa, in late September, Michelle Obama declared that "Iowa will make the difference. ... If Barack doesn't win Iowa, it is just a dream. If we win Iowa, then we can move to the world as it should be." Such candor was unwelcome among political professionals, and Obama's campaign immediately moved to tamp down expectations. But

those following the race closely knew she spoke the truth.

The Jefferson-Jackson dinner, a mammoth Iowa Democratic fundraiser in November, was a marquee event featuring the six leading Democratic candidates, and it proved to be a key moment. The dinner, which each year drew Democrats from across the state, traditionally opened the final phase of the Iowa campaign. It was a chance for each candidate to impress important political players. Some 9,000 people attended the dinner in 2007, but Obama's supporters stood out as the loudest, most energetic and by far the most numerous. From the cheap seats in the balconies, youthful Obama supporters wearing distinctive red T-shirts shouted back and forth across the hall. "Fired

Up!" yelled one side. "Ready to go!" answered the other.

In the lead-up to the dinner, Clinton had uncharacteristically stumbled. During a debate in Philadelphia she was unable to say clearly whether she favored driver's licenses for illegal immigrants. She also waffled on a question about the release of archival material from the Clinton presidency. The exchanges turned her cautious style into a liability, reviving memories of the parsing answers the Clintons had given during their White House scandal years. At the dinner itself, Obama was the last candidate to speak, not taking the stage until 11 p.m. He invoked Martin Luther King's "fierce urgency of now," a quotation that became a signature phrase. He offered a passionate call to Democratic principles and drew sharp contrasts with Clinton, whom he portrayed, without naming her, as driven more by calculation than conviction. "The same old Washington textbook campaigns just won't do in this election. That's why not answering questions because we are afraid our answers won't be popular just won't do," Obama said. "If we are really serious about winning this election, Democrats, we can't live in fear of losing it." The next morning The Des Moines Register's political columnist, David Yepsen, an influential voice in the state, praised the speech as a potential turning point in the campaign. The address provided the framework for countless stump speeches as Obama traveled the snowy country roads around Iowa for appearances in local school gymnasiums, American Legion posts, church halls and community centers.

Then talk show host Oprah Winfrey joined Obama for a three-state tour in December, including two stops in Iowa, reinforcing the aura of excitement around his campaign and drawing crowds of 18,000 in Des Moines and 10,000 in Cedar Rapids despite sleet and snow. Requiring people to give their names and contact information to get their free tickets to the events generated a formidable list of potential new supporters. A few days before the caucus, The Des Moines Register poll shook up the political landscape by showing Obama with a significant lead. And on caucus night itself, young voters and independents, Obama's core supporters, turned out in record numbers. About twice as many people participated in the Democratic caucuses as had in 2004, the previous high mark. The result was a blowout: Obama finished far ahead of any of his rivals. Clinton came in third, just behind former Sen. John Edwards.

Sen. Obama enters a school gymnasium for an event in Clinton, Iowa, in December 2007.

In the giddy days that followed, it seemed to many that Obama would quickly wrap up the nomination. The Clinton campaign had always viewed the New Hampshire primary five days later as a "firewall," because the former first lady had led there for months. But Obama surged after his Iowa win, and soon New Hampshire polls gave him a substantial lead in that state also. But now it was Clinton's turn to defy expectations, and when the votes were counted in New Hampshire, Clinton won. It was a narrow victory, not the decisive one her campaign had originally hoped for, but a victory nonetheless. And women voters, who had sided with Obama in Iowa, this time showed a clear preference for Clinton, a pattern that would persist. "I come here tonight with a very full heart," Clinton said in declaring victory. "I listened to you, and in the process I found my own voice."

Obama watched the disappointing numbers roll in alongside his wife, Michelle, his sister Auma, and Valerie Jarrett, an adviser and close family friend. "People were in shock. We were not prepared for it," Jarrett said. Obama went quietly from person to person. When he got to Jarrett, he put his hands on her shoulders and looked her in the face. "This will prove to be a good thing," Obama said. "We are going to have to redouble our efforts." The divided results in the first two contests foreshadowed tumultuous weeks ahead, with Obama and Clinton trading victories and splitting the vote.

In the Nevada caucuses, Clinton won more votes, but due to the Democrats' complex system, Obama eventually gained three more delegates. Next came South Carolina. As Obama's advisers had hoped, he won a resounding victory from the heavily black Democratic electorate, defeating Clinton 2-1. Obama received another big boost in the days that followed, as Sen. Edward Kennedy, a hero of the liberal establishment and the guardian of the legacy of the martyred Kennedy brothers, endorsed Obama, along with Caroline Kennedy, the only living child of President John F. Kennedy. If the Democratic Party had a royal family, it was the Kennedys. Many Democrats had yearned for decades for a restoration of the promise that was seemingly lost with the assassinations of John and Robert Kennedy. Since the day Obama stepped onto the national stage at the 2004 Democratic convention, the parallels with Jack and Bobby had been part of the excitement surrounding him. Now the most prominent members of the Kennedy family were publicly declaring him a worthy heir to Camelot. Caroline Kennedy even wrote a newspaper article with the headline "A President Like My Father." Caroline Kennedy, Ted Kennedy and the senator's son, Patrick Kennedy, a congressman from Rhode Island,

gathered onstage with Obama at American University, site of a famous speech by President Kennedy, a tableau that dominated television imagery for days. In the lead-up to Super Tuesday—Feb. 5, the day almost half the primary states would cast their votes—the Kennedys traveled the country extolling Obama's candidacy.

Back when Barack and Michelle Obama were first meeting with advisers to consider a presidential run, Super Tuesday had loomed in the future like a forbidding brick wall. The enormous voting day was thought to heavily favor Hillary Clinton, because it was extraordinarily expensive to run television ads in so many states and she was by far the better-known candidate — especially in New York and California, the day's biggest prizes. But David Plouffe, an Obama adviser who became his campaign manager, argued that Super Tuesday need not be a roadblock. Because party rules awarded delegates proportionally in a system based on congressional districts, Clinton could win New York and California and still not roll up a significant lead. The Obama campaign would pick up plenty of delegates itself in those states by winning individual districts. Meanwhile, Obama could use his field organization and enthusiastic following to run up large margins in other states.

That's essentially how it happened. Super Tuesday, the day the Obama campaign feared the most, ended in a draw. Clinton won the grand prizes of California and New York, as expected, while Obama took more states around the country. But by failing to knock him off, Clinton opened the door to Obama's strategy of steadily accumulating delegates through small states and caucuses. It was not apparent at the time, but Obama essentially won the Democratic nomination on Super Tuesday, simply by surviving.

But it would be a mistake to attribute Obama's success solely to strategic vision and tactical skill. Without an extraordinary candidate, even the most brilliant strategic plan would have failed. As the primary battle moved from state to state, both campaigns endlessly analyzed and subdivided the electorate, trying to understand why blue-collar voters, for example, were suspicious of Obama and younger voters were devoted to him. But beyond this analysis, it was clear that something in Obama's identity and message had struck an unusual chord, energizing large groups in ways that had not been seen for years. Most obviously, voters responded to his emphasis on change, a message he adopted in part out of necessity, because he could hardly run on his lengthy résumé. By chance or not, Obama had clearly hit a nerve, and virtually every other candidate — not just Clinton, but also John McCain and Mitt Romney, watching nervously

Obama fans show their support in Milwaukee in February 2008.

from the Republican sidelines — adopted some version of a "change" slogan, though it was hard for such establishment figures to argue that they represented something new.

After Super Tuesday, the Clinton campaign was broke. Clinton had been forced to lend her campaign $5 million in the days leading up to the coast-to-coast primary, hoping for a conclusive victory that would knock Obama out of the race. Less than a week afterward, Clinton ousted her campaign manager and longtime aide Patti Solis Doyle, and in the next two weeks Obama racked up 10 straight victories, running up a big lead in delegates that he would never relinquish. As the contest moved toward major primaries in Texas and Ohio at the beginning of March, the primary fight had lasted far longer than anyone had anticipated. Some Democrats grumbled that Clinton should withdraw so the party could unify around Obama. Clinton's husband, the politically savvy former president, gave public

expression to the campaign's predicament. "If she wins Texas and Ohio, I think she will be the nominee," Bill Clinton told a crowd in Beaumont, Texas. "If you don't deliver for her, then I don't think she can be. It's all on you." The former president had put a rosy spin on it, but the stakes were clear. Clinton, the overwhelming favorite just a few months earlier, had to win both states just to remain in the race.

Following page
Supporters in Des Moines demonstrate their enthusiasm by making an "O" — for Obama — with their arms before the senator's speech in January 2008.

9 *"This is our moment":*
Getting the nomination

THE TENSE MUSIC and dark lighting infused the images of children nestled in their beds with a mood of foreboding. "It's 3 a.m., and your children are safe and asleep. But there's a phone in the White House, and it's ringing," a narrator said ominously. "Something's happening in the world. Your vote will decide who answers that call — whether it's someone who already knows the world's leaders, knows the military, someone tested and ready to lead in a dangerous world." Darkness turned to light as a businesslike Hillary Clinton appeared onscreen and picked up the phone. This provocative television spot began running in Texas four days before the critical primaries there and in Ohio. The message was as clear as it was powerful:

Obama greets the crowd before a town hall meeting in Lancaster, Pa., in March 2008.

Barack Obama was a neophyte who could not be trusted with the most basic of presidential duties, protecting the nation. The line of attack was risky, since its raw, heavy-handed tone could backfire. But Clinton's plight at this point approached desperation.

The attack on Obama's readiness resonated with many voters. His exciting youthfulness came with a price, a relative lack of national government experience that was his greatest vulnerability. Sensing an advantage, Clinton amplified her message at a rally in Waco, Texas, surrounding herself with retired military leaders and questioning Obama's qualifications to be commander in chief. She belittled his national security experience as consisting of "a speech at an anti-war rally," hitting back at his claim that his early opposition to the Iraq War was proof of sound judgment. Clinton noted that she, in contrast, had traveled to more than 80 countries, recalling one trip to Bosnia as first lady when the welcoming ceremony "had to be moved inside because of sniper fire." That turned out to be untrue, causing her campaign great embarrassment, but that was later.

If Obama won Ohio or Texas, Clinton would likely be forced from the race and the nomination would be his. Instead, bolstered by the "3 a.m." ads and Obama's own missteps, Clinton won both primaries on March 4. Obama, in rueful comments afterward, acknowledged that his enormous campaign rallies before the vote had actually hurt his campaign, suggesting a remoteness and leaving his message "stale."

That set the stage for the race that followed. In capturing Ohio and Texas, Clinton had emphatically halted Obama's 10-contest winning streak and put an end to several weeks of headlines about his rolling successes. At the same time, a pattern was emerging. Obama was winning caucuses, where field organization was especially important, as well as Western states and those with large black populations. Clinton was winning big states with many blue-collar voters. There were exceptions to these trends, but neither candidate was making decisive inroads into the other's turf. Obama's winning streak had given him a big enough lead in delegates that Clinton probably could not catch up, but it was not big enough to eliminate her mathematically. Obama realized he was in for a long fight. The morning after the Texas and Ohio primaries, he stopped to talk to the reporters on his campaign plane before it took off from San Antonio. Heading back to his seat in the first-class cabin, Obama warned the journalists not to expect to see much of home. "I think we're going to be on the road a few more weeks, guys," he said. A reporter shouted out, "Is it going to be weeks or months?" Obama just smiled and kept walking.

Race had always been a theme of the election, but it had been a subterranean one so far, rarely emerging as a central issue. That was a success for Obama, whose strategy involved minimizing overt discussions of race that could pigeonhole him and polarize the electorate. It had been an extraordinary feat for an African-American to perform so well in a largely white country. But as the campaign dragged on and the Clintons mounted an aggressive counterattack, a racial divide was beginning to emerge, with white Democrats moving toward Clinton as blacks remained firmly loyal to Obama. In Ohio and Texas, unlike Iowa and New Hampshire, white voters had sided with Clinton by large margins. In the Mississippi primary a week later, the racial differences were startling, with white voters favoring Clinton 3-1 and 90 percent of blacks supporting Obama. This was something of a low point for a candidate who had started his campaign by showing a unique ability to attract whites and blacks alike. Would the country now fall back into old patterns, threatening Obama's promise of rising above history? It is true that white Democrats in Mississippi were among the most conservative in the nation, making them natural Clinton supporters. Nonetheless it was hard not to wonder if the post-racial magic was fading. In a national Pew Research poll, 20 percent of white Democrats said they would defect and support John McCain if Obama were nominated. Those numbers were no doubt exaggerated, and probably by a good margin, because the poll was taken in the heat of a bitter primary contest. But the finding was nonetheless sobering.

THE PASTOR PROBLEM

Two days after the Mississippi primary, ABC's "Good Morning America" aired video excerpts of incendiary sermons by Obama's longtime Chicago pastor, Rev. Jeremiah Wright. "The government gives them [African-Americans] the drugs, builds bigger prisons, passes a three-strikes law and then wants us to sing 'God bless America?' No, no, no. Not God bless America, God damn America," Wright declared in what became the most infamous clip. He also seemed to say the U.S. had sown the seeds of the Sept. 11 attacks and that the government had fostered the spread of AIDS. Obama quickly condemned the remarks as "appalling," but Wright's sermons cut to the core of his political appeal. Since he had first appeared on the national stage in 2004, Obama had presented himself as a unifying, non-threatening figure who could help heal the country's racial divisions. The last thing he needed was to be associated with a black leader who bitterly condemned white America. He was to be a new, conciliatory kind of candidate, a new kind of black leader. Wright's sound bites risked instantly undoing all that. It was a perilous moment. The next day, March 14, Obama visited the Chicago Tribune's editorial board for a previously scheduled meeting, and he argued that the video clips did not accurately reflect Wright's message. "In fairness to him, this was sort of a greatest hits," Obama said, adding quickly, "That doesn't excuse them." He spoke of Wright as a member of the 1960s generation. "You know, I can completely just disown it and say I don't understand it," Obama said. "But I do understand it." He also took on recent comments by Geraldine Ferraro, a Clinton supporter, suggesting that Obama's success in the race was due to the fact that he was African-American. "The idea that 'Oh, you know, let's get a black guy in there,' I think, just doesn't make sense," Obama said.

With the Wright videos dominating the airwaves, Obama had to take action. At a rally in Pennsylvania, he uncharacteristically ended his comments with "God bless America," an implicit rebuke to Wright. At an Obama campaign event in an Indianapolis suburb, the crowd was led in prayer, also a rarity. But these were small gestures. Obama told his fellow Illinois senator, Dick Durbin, that he planned to deliver a major address on race, that he had given it a lot of deep thought and personal attention. As the day approached, the prospect of the first viable black presidential candidate confronting America's racial history created a sense of drama. Obama chose Philadelphia's National Constitution Center as his site, and unlike many of his addresses, its tone was not lofty and impassioned but subdued and analytical, almost anguished. He suggested that whites and blacks had a rough symmetry of anger, prejudice and legitimate grievance. Even while criticizing Wright's comments, he sought to put them in perspective, but a perspective that did not blame whites alone. "I can no more disown [Wright] than I can disown the black community," Obama said. "I can no more disown him than I can my white grandmother — a woman who helped raise me, a woman who sacrificed again and again for me, a woman who loves me as much as she loves anything in this world, but a woman who once confessed her fear of black men who passed by her on the street, and who on more than one occasion has uttered racial or ethnic stereotypes that made me cringe."

Some praised the talk as the best political speech in years, and it succeeded in bringing the immediate crisis to a close. But it was impossible to know how many voters had been permanently turned off by the Wright sermons, and whether the public's impressions of a candidate whose history was still relatively little-known had been seriously damaged.

That would be tested relatively soon in the upcoming primary in Pennsylvania, a place once memorably described by political consultant James Carville as Pittsburgh and Philadelphia with Alabama in between.

Obama continued struggling to attract blue-collar voters, who made up a big part of the Pennsylvania electorate, and it was unclear what role racial issues were playing. Obama threw himself into courting these voters. He ratcheted up an us-against-them populism that fed on the grievances of working-class families. Among the first television ads he aired in Pennsylvania was a commercial excoriating Exxon Mobil for its $40 billion profit the previous year. A President Obama, he promised, would make oil companies "pay a penalty" with a windfall profits tax. He visited blue-collar workplaces and hangouts. He shook hands at a steel plant during a shift change. He visited the factory floor of a wire manufacturer and walked among giant coils of cable while steam rose from vats behind him. He dropped by sports bars to watch the NCAA basketball tournament and hoist a brew. He shoved a hot dog in his mouth. And he went bowling, though his performance was memorably poor, with a score of 37 that became the butt of jokes on late-night television.

Obama seemed to be feeling the stress. There did not appear to be anything he could do to win over white working-class voters. If he could do that in just one big state, he could probably end the primary fight once and for all. Instead, Clinton's argument that she was winning the big swing states, and was therefore better positioned to take on the Republicans in the fall, was frustratingly difficult to disprove. One way Obama dealt with the tension was to exercise regularly. He spent one morning workout session in Erie, for example, alone with his personal assistant in a hotel gym room. Listening to his iPod and scanning a morning paper, he bounced between a treadmill and an exercise bike. Obama shut out reporters from these workout sessions, despite many requests to view them. "That's sort of my quiet time," he said. "If you start having a bunch of reporters there, then it's not quiet time." The day before the Pennsylvania primary, Obama appeared in Scranton at the Glider Diner to schmooze with the patrons, a classic campaign appearance. He listened to a trumpet solo by a 17-year-old who had been waiting for hours to perform for him, and he signed excuse notes for two students—"Excuse Colin!" "Excuse Joey!"— who had skipped high school to meet him. But as Obama tucked into one more breakfast he probably didn't want, one of the cluster of reporters that always surrounded him now called out a foreign policy question. "Why can't I just eat my waffle?" Obama responded plaintively.

Despite outspending Clinton 3-1, Obama decisively lost the Pennsylvania primary. The outcome showcased the frustrations of both candidates. Obama had a significant, if small, lead in delegates, but could not close the deal and turn his attention to his Republican rival. This was becoming one of the longest, most bruising primary

Top left: Michelle and Barack Obama eat cheesesteaks at Pat's
King of Steaks in Philadelphia in April 2008.

Above: Obama returns bowling shoes at the Pleasant Valley
Bowling Center in Altoona, Pa., in March 2008. His score was
37 after bowling seven frames.

Bottom left: Independent vendors in Pittsburgh sell Obama
merchandise before an event in March 2008.

battles in recent history. For Clinton's part, her 10-point victory in Pennsylvania was, once again, not big enough to significantly diminish Obama's lead in delegates. She came away from the state with only 12 more delegates than he did and an even steeper uphill climb in the remaining contests. The strategy outlined so carefully by Obama's advisers at the campaign's outset was being realized with remarkable precision. He had built enough of an early lead that, given the Democratic Party's proportional delegate rules, no matter how many times Clinton won impressive victories in big states, she never seemed to be able to catch up.

Both candidates soldiered on, but the end was near. The next round of big primaries came on May 6 in North Carolina and Indiana. In a rare decision, Obama allowed network news cameras to capture him playing basketball in Kokomo, Ind. Obama was a basketball enthusiast, but campaign staffers were initially reluctant to show him playing a sport heavily associated with African-Americans. The game's importance to Obama was illustrated by the fact that he had played basketball on nearly every day there was a primary vote. The sport has an almost religious status in Indiana, and Obama was doing all he could to keep Clinton from scoring a big victory in the state, so this time he let in the cameras. It was no coincidence, perhaps, that the sight of Obama vigorously trotting up and down the court created a contrast with Republican John McCain, who was 71. Still, in an interview with the Chicago Tribune, Obama promised not to use McCain's age against him. "I don't think that's going to be the issue that people vote on," Obama said. "People respect John McCain. They know he's a tough guy. He's gone through things that I think most of us can only imagine."

Obama did well in those primaries—well enough, at least. He won a resounding victory in North Carolina, as expected given its sizable African-American population, while Clinton eked out only a bare majority in Indiana, where the demographics, and the state's political establishment, had favored her. This effectively ended the contest. The campaign continued for another month, with the demographic divide between the candidates persisting. Women, the elderly and white working-class voters favored Clinton; blacks, the young and the college-educated favored Obama. Each candidate prevailed in the states where the makeup of the electorate worked in his or her favor. But the formidable lead in delegates that Obama built up through his string of victories in February proved decisive. Obama clinched the nomination on June 3, when primaries were held by the last two states — South Dakota, which Clinton won, and Montana, which he won. With Obama leading in delegates elected by voters, a slew of superdelegates — the party leaders and elected officials who attend the convention — endorsed the Illinois

senator, providing him a guaranteed majority. In a bit of political theater, Obama traveled to St. Paul to claim his status as the party's presumptive nominee in the same arena where Republicans were scheduled to hold their convention in September.

"WHERE WE GO FROM HERE"
As he flew from Chicago's Midway Airport to the Twin Cities, the mood aboard the campaign plane was festive, with Obama standing in the forward section chatting with campaign staffers who had wanted to be along for the historic night. Joining him were his wife, Michelle, as well as a half-dozen associates from Chicago. The group included Valerie Jarrett, a close friend an adviser, and two basketball-playing buddies, Eric Whitaker and Marty Nesbitt, who was often called Obama's best friend. Hyatt hotel heiress Penny Pritzker, Obama's national finance chairwoman, was also there. The candidate, who had become quite reserved when it came to reporters, did not come to the journalists' section of the plane, but David Axelrod, his top message-crafter, summed up the candidate's feelings. "One of the things about Sen. Obama, and we've learned this throughout this campaign, is that he is, you know, he never gets too high and he never gets too low," Axelrod said. "When we've faced challenges he's been very steady. And when we have things to celebrate, he's happy. But he understands that there are challenges ahead as well. And he's already thinking about where we go from here. But he's obviously very happy. He's worked very hard, and he's earned this."

A few hours later Obama stepped onto the stage at Xcel Energy Center arena to claim his prize after a primary season that had dragged on through 16 months and 54 contests. "Tonight, I can stand before you and say that I will be the Democratic nominee for president of the United States," Obama said. He offered a lavish tribute to Hillary Clinton, whose supporters he would need badly in the fall. He took a few well-aimed jabs at his Republican opponent, McCain, on whom he was now free to unleash all his resources. And he launched into the sort of oratory that had brought him to that night. "America, this is our moment," Obama said. "This is our time... If we are willing to work for it, and fight for it, and believe in it, then I am absolutely certain that generations from now, we will be able to look back and tell our children that this was the moment when we began to provide care for the sick and good jobs to the jobless; this was the moment when the rise of the oceans began to slow and our planet began to heal; this was the moment when we ended a war and secured our nation and restored our image as the last, best hope on Earth."

Barack Obama had come remarkably far in four years.

Democratic presidential candidate Sen. Hillary Clinton speaks at New York's Baruch College on June 3, 2008. Although Clinton did not concede that night, Obama had gathered enough delegates to claim the title of presumptive Democratic nominee. Clinton congratulated Obama and his campaign and thanked her staff and supporters. Following page: On the same day, in St. Paul, Barack Obama told the crowd: "Tonight I can stand before you and say that I will be the Democratic nominee for president of the United States."

He was the first African-American presidential nominee of a major party. He had shown the sort of ability to stir audiences that had not been seen in decades. In 2004, Obama had been unknown to most Americans until he delivered a spectacular address at the Democratic National Convention. That speech had inspired many people to muse, some only half-seriously, that Obama could be America's first black president. But no one thought it could happen in four years, that Obama would go from being the keynoter at one convention to the candidate at the next. When Obama had started his 2004 campaign for U.S. Senate, he had been a long shot by a considerable margin, but his toughest rivals had self-destructed. When he decided to seek the Democratic nomination against Hillary Clinton, the odds also had

been against him. But by some combination of luck and talent, serendipity and charisma, Obama had come, essentially out of the clear blue, to lead the Democratic Party in a year when the Democrats were widely expected to win the presidency. Few things were entirely new in American politics, but this came close. Now there was one final task. Obama still confronted a political map that gave the Republicans considerable advantages, though he was to waste little time trying to redraw it. He still faced an electorate that was sharply divided, though it was more Democratic than it had been for years. And he still needed to campaign in a country that, from its creation, had been traveling a difficult journey toward racial reconciliation. What was unclear was how far along that path America had come. Obama, like the rest of us, was about to find out.

10 On the issues

AFTER a hard-fought primary campaign, Sen. Barack Obama moved to the center in some of his positions. He angered some supporters when he voted in the summer of 2008 to expand the government's wiretapping powers and criticized a Supreme Court decision in June overturning the death penalty for a child rapist. During his years in the Illinois Senate and since being elected to the U.S. Senate, Obama has had a mostly liberal voting record. Facing a general election contest, he took a more centrist position on foreign policy, trade and other issues.

Obama's position

THE WAR IN IRAQ

Like no other, this was the issue that propelled Obama through the early months of a primary campaign where many of the leading candidates had voted to support an invasion. As he prepared to run for the U.S. Senate in 2004, Obama had given a speech in Chicago in 2002 against the invasion. He constantly reminded activists of it as he campaigned in Iowa and New Hampshire. Obama was critical of the "surge" that some have credited with making Iraq more secure. He has called for a 16-month timetable for withdrawal of combat troops, which he has said he would start as soon as taking office.

THE WAR ON TERROR

Obama has called for a clear set of federal regulations for chemical plants that would enhance security and safety training. He has also called for improved tracking of spent fuel rods from nuclear power plants. Seeking to keep drinking water safe, Obama has called for upgrades in monitoring and security efforts. He believes the central front on the war against terrorism is Afghanistan, not Iraq.

THE MILITARY

Obama maintains that the nation's military is a "20th Century structure" despite facing "21st Century problems." He believes such things as special operations forces, civil affairs and information operations must be built up. He supports plans to increase the size of the Army by 65,000 soldiers and the Marines by 27,000 troops. Obama has committed to a review of each major defense program, while also maintaining that "unparalleled airpower" remains essential. He supports missile defense, as long as it is developed in a way that is "pragmatic and cost-effective."

McCain's position

THE WAR IN IRAQ

Sen. John McCain was among the members of Congress who, in October 2002, supported the use of U.S. military force against Iraq. McCain became a critic of the early conduct of the war, ultimately voicing a loss of confidence in Defense Secretary Donald Rumsfeld. McCain supported the "surge" in forces President Bush ordered in January 2007 and credits it with making Iraq more secure. He maintains that U.S. forces must remain there until Iraq can defend itself, and has called a decades-long commitment of U.S. forces there acceptable so long as Americans aren't suffering casualties

THE WAR ON TERROR

The terrorist attacks of Sept. 11, 2001, "represented more than a failure of intelligence," McCain says. They underscored a failure of national policy in the face of a growing global network of terrorism. He pushed for and supported the 9/11 Commission that investigated the attacks. McCain maintains a commitment to a war against "violent Islamic extremists" on all fronts "using all instruments of national power." This includes engagement with enemies "on the battlefield of ideas." McCain has pledged to hunt down Osama bin Laden — "to the gates of hell" if necessary.

THE MILITARY

McCain supports an enlargement of the U.S. military "to meet new challenges to our security." He supports an increase in deployment of U.S. forces in Afghanistan. The military also must be funded under the routine budget of the federal government, he believes, as opposed to the repeated emergency appropriations that have financed the wars in Iraq and Afghanistan. To guard against the threats of hostile nations, he supports the creation of new missile defenses such as the missile battery in Poland and radar network in the Czech Republic that the Bush administration has promoted.

Obama's position

▌ TAXES

Obama has called for tax relief for 150 million workers through a "Making Work Pay" tax credit of up to $500 per person, or $1,000 per working family. His campaign says the tax credit would completely eliminate income taxes for 10 million Americans. He would also eliminate income taxes for seniors making less than $50,000 a year. Obama wants the Bush administration's tax cuts for those who make more than $250,000 a year eliminated and would extend and index the Alternative Minimum Tax patch, something that keeps it from applying to even more taxpayers than it already does.

▌ SPENDING

Obama has proposed billions in spending to create jobs and enhance government programs to help the less fortunate. He plans to fund those by ending the Iraq War, eliminating corporate tax breaks and raising taxes on those with higher incomes. Obama says he believes in pay-as-you-go budgeting rules that require new spending initiatives or tax changes to be paid for by cuts to other programs or new revenue. He has pushed for more disclosure and transparency for earmarks. Obama urges the elimination of subsidies for oil and gas companies and has pledged to tackle wasteful spending in Medicare.

▌ GAS PRICES

Although the idea of a "holiday" from the federal gas tax was quickly endorsed by Sen. Hillary Clinton, who was desperately trying to slow Obama's progress in winning the nomination, Obama objected, calling it a "gimmick," even though it was popular with many voters facing surging pump prices. In early August, Obama altered his position on tapping the nation's Strategic Petroleum Reserve to help relieve gas prices. That move came just days after Obama softened his position on the expansion of oil drilling along the nation's coastline.

McCain's position

▌ TAXES

McCain opposed the first round of Bush tax cuts as too heavily weighted toward the wealthy but supported an acceleration of the cuts in 2003 and the final tax bill in 2006. He also backs a continuation of the Bush tax cuts. He proposes a permanent repeal of the Alternative Minimum Tax and promises to cut taxes for the middle class and corporations. He has promised to avert new taxes if he is elected and would like to see a 60 percent vote requirement in Congress for any new taxes. He supports a ban on Internet taxes. And he has pledged to pursue a "simpler" alternative to the existing federal income tax.

▌ SPENDING

McCain pledges to ban the earmarks that enable members of Congress to slip spending for special projects back home into federal spending bills. He vows to "make their authors famous," promising presidential vetoes of "pork-barrel" spending. He has proposed a one-year halt in the increase of "discretionary" federal spending to make a "top-to-bottom review" of all federal programs. Facing a near-record federal budget deficit, in which government spending now exceeds revenue by more than $400 billion a year, McCain says he "will not leave office without balancing the federal budget."

▌ GAS PRICES

The senator has supported a summer "holiday" from the federal gas tax, suggesting that holding the 18.4-cents-per-gallon tax in abeyance from Memorial Day to Labor Day could help ease the burden on consumers from prices that soared to over $4 per gallon this summer. He has pledged to stop filling the federal Strategic Petroleum Reserve to ease pressure on oil prices. He has proposed lifting a longtime federal ban against oil drilling on the Outer Continental Shelf, to make more oil available. He has proposed to eliminate policies that contribute to higher transportation and food costs — including a federal subsidy for the production of ethanol.

Obama's position

McCain's position

▌ENERGY

Obama has pledged to create 5 million new jobs by investing $150 billion over the next decade to build cleaner energy generation. He has called for a national goal within 10 years of saving more oil than is now imported from the Middle East and Venezuela combined. He wants to see 1 million plug-in hybrid cars capable of getting up to 150 miles per gallon on the road by 2015. Obama wants to ensure that 10 percent of electricity comes from renewable sources by 2012, with a full quarter of it coming from those sources by 2025.

In addition to permitting oil and natural gas exploration and production on the Outer Continental Shelf, McCain proposes reducing dependence on foreign oil. He suggests a "Clean Car Challenge" for U.S. automakers: Offering a $5,000 tax credit for purchases of "zero carbon emission" cars and encouraging automakers to be first to market with such vehicles. He proposes a $300 million federal prize for the manufacture of a significantly improved car battery. He supports the advancement of clean coal in power generation and vows to put the U.S. on track toward 45 new nuclear power plants by 2030.

▌SOCIAL SECURITY

Obama supports making some with higher incomes pay more in Social Security taxes, specifically those making more than $250,000 annually, or roughly the top 3 percent of income earners. The 6.2 percent payroll tax is now applied to wages up to $102,000 a year. Obama's plan would not increase the tax on wages between that amount and $250,000.

McCain maintains that any solution to the economic imbalance in the Social Security system must be a bipartisan plan. And he has pledged that he "will not leave office without fixing the problems that threaten our future prosperity." He has supported President Bush's proposal for personal retirement savings plans as a supplement to the long-standing federal payroll tax deductions financing Social Security. McCain has maintained that he opposes any increase in the payroll tax to fix Social Security but has said that, in the spirit of bipartisan negotiations, "There is nothing that's off the table."

▌HOUSING

Citing his experience with the issue in Chicago, Obama has pledged to crack down on mortgage fraud. He would create a "Universal Mortgage Credit" for homeowners who do not itemize on their tax returns. For home buyers, he wants to create a Homeowner Obligation Made Explicit score, which would provide potential borrowers with a simplified, standardized metric to help compare various mortgage products and understand the full cost of a loan.

In the face of a home mortgage foreclosure crisis, McCain has proposed a "HOME Plan" to enable "deserving" families "to trade a burdensome mortgage" for a loan more reflective of their home's value. Those who secured non-conventional mortgages after 2005 and cannot meet the payments but are credit-worthy could apply for a new 30-year fixed-rate mortgage. He also would form a Department of Justice task force to investigate criminal wrongdoing in the mortgage industry. McCain, calling the estate tax a "death tax," supports raising its exemption from taxation to estates valued at up to $10 million while cutting the tax rate.

Obama's position

McCain's position

▌HEALTH CARE

Obama would make available a new national health plan to all Americans, including the self-employed and small businesses. He often tells audiences that they will be able to buy affordable health coverage that is similar to the plan available to members of Congress. Under his plan, eligibility would be guaranteed and subsidies would be available for those who do not qualify for Medicaid. Although coverage for children would be required, he stops short of universal coverage.

He opposes a new government-financed system of health care for the 47 million Americans who are uninsured, and voted against extending prescription drug benefits to Medicare patients. He hopes to make private health insurance more affordable. He supports relief in the tax code, including a tax credit of $2,500 for individuals and $5,000 for families, to offset the cost of private health insurance for those not covered by employers. He wants health insurance to go from job to job. He proposes expanding the benefits of Health Savings Accounts that enable people to set aside money tax-free.

▌EDUCATION

The senator has called for a "Zero to Five" plan that would provide support to children and parents, stressing early care and education for infants. He would expand Early Head Start and Head Start and pledges to provide affordable, high-quality child care for working families. Obama often talks about reforming the federal No Child Left Behind program and providing more school funding. He has promised to do more to recruit, prepare, retain and reward teachers. Although he sends his children to a private school, he opposes vouchers for those who select to send their kids to private schools.

The senator has supported the No Child Left Behind legislation of the Bush administration, which requires annual testing in public schools to ensure "adequate yearly progress" is being made. "This age of honest reporting" has exposed which schools are succeeding and which ones are failing, he believes. In addition, he says, any child in a school that fails to improve should be able to change schools. And he wants to empower parents to send their children to private schools if public schools are insufficient. A supporter of school choice, he has backed federal tuition vouchers to assist parents.

▌IMMIGRATION

Obama says he wants to "preserve the integrity of our borders" and supports additional personnel, infrastructure and technology at the border and ports of entry. He would work to remove incentives to illegally enter the country by cracking down on employers who hire undocumented immigrants. He also supports a system that allows undocumented immigrants in good standing to pay a fine, learn English and then "go to the back of the line" for the opportunity to become citizens. By working to promote economic development in Mexico, he believes, illegal immigration could be reduced.

The Republican senator, along with Democratic co-sponsors in the Senate, has supported "comprehensive immigration reform." This includes not only a strengthening of borders, but also offering those who qualify, among an estimated 12 million or more illegal immigrants already in the U.S., a path toward legal residence and potential citizenship. "As president," McCain promises, "I will secure the border." In addition, he would enable workers who entered the U.S. illegally but have found jobs, learned English and avoided further criminal wrongdoing to seek a path to citizenship. America will always be that "shining city upon a hill," McCain says.

Obama's position

CLIMATE CHANGE

Obama has proposed an economy-wide cap-and-trade program to reduce greenhouse gas emissions 80 percent by 2050. The system would allow pollution credits to be auctioned, with proceeds used to invest in clean energy. Obama says he would re-engage with the UN Framework Convention on Climate Change, the main international forum dedicated to addressing the climate problem. He would also create a Global Energy Forum of the world's largest emitters to focus exclusively on global energy and environmental issues.

FAMILY ISSUES

Obama often stresses that people who work full time should not live in poverty. He would further raise the minimum wage and index it to inflation, while also significantly increasing the Earned Income Tax Credit. Obama would also seek to require employers to provide seven sick days per year and expand the Family and Medical Leave Act. He supports legalized abortion.

FIREARMS

Obama offered a guarded response in June 2008, when the Supreme Court struck down the District of Columbia's prohibition on handguns and sidestepped providing a view on the 32-year-old local gun ban. His carefully worded statement applauded the court for providing "much-needed guidance to local jurisdictions." Obama said he has "always believed that the 2nd Amendment protects the right of individuals to bear arms, but I also identify with the need for crime-ravaged communities to save their children from the violence that plagues our streets through common-sense, effective safety measures." He would re-establish the assault weapons ban.

McCain's position

McCain acknowledges the impact of man-made emissions on global warming. He believes they can be curbed with a market-based system of "caps and trades." He proposes setting limits on greenhouse gas emissions and allowing businesses to buy and sell rights to emit pollutants. Any company that could reduce its emissions could sell emissions rights to others. He proposes a timetable for cutting emissions of greenhouse gases in the U.S. by more than half: Returning emissions to 2005 levels by 2012, and taking emissions back to 1990 levels by 2050. This would amount to a 66 percent reduction, he says.

Calling abortion "a human tragedy," McCain has urged the U.S. Supreme Court to overturn the 1973 Roe vs. Wade ruling that legalized it. He supports adoption and with his wife adopted an orphan. He thinks adoption is best for the traditional couple of a man and woman but suggests the question of gay adoption is best left to the states. He opposes a constitutional amendment banning gay marriage. But he argues that federal courts should not overturn state legislation "to preserve the traditional family." And he has promised to appoint federal judges who won't be "legislating from the bench."

Professing "a sacred duty to protect" the constitutional right to keep and bear arms, McCain also maintains that the government has an obligation to keep firearms out of the hands of criminals. He opposes holding gun manufacturers liable for the commission of crimes and has voted against federal bans on private ownership of assault rifles. He has supported legislation requiring gunmakers to include safety devices such as trigger locks with the weapons. He supports instant criminal background checks for gun buyers, including those at gun shows. But McCain has opposed a waiting period for people buying firearms.

Afterword

June 3, 2008, Obama campaign headquarters on Michigan Avenue in Chicago.

Credits and sources

CHICAGO TRIBUNE
EDITOR   Gerould W. Kern
MANAGING EDITOR, FEATURES   James Warren

OBAMA:
The Essential Guide to the Democratic Nominee

EDITOR   Naftali Bendavid
ART DIRECTOR   Joan Cairney
PHOTO EDITOR   Andrew Johnston
COPY EDITOR   Valentina Djeljosevic
RESEARCHER   Lelia Boyd Arnheim
IMAGING TECHNICIAN   Christine Bruno
PROJECT MANAGERS   Chuck Burke, Bill Parker and Susan Zukrow

Introduction: The phenomenon
Interview with J. Ann Selzer July 2, 2008
Some material taken from "It would not have been possible 40 years ago," Mike Dorning, Chicago Tribune, June 4, 2008

1. "A mind in full tilt"
This chapter is based largely on "Family portraits: Strong personalities shaped a future senator, Barack Obama," Tim Jones, Chicago Tribune, March 27, 2007
New York World quotation cited in Michael Kazin, "A Godly Hero: The Life of William Jennings Bryan" (2006)
Material also taken from "Obama to give keynote address," Jill Zuckman and David Mendell, Chicago Tribune, July 15, 2004

2. "A race thing"
This chapter is based largely on "The not-so-simple story of Barack Obama's youth; Shaped by different worlds, an outsider found ways to fit in," Kirsten Scharnberg and Kim Barker, Chicago Tribune, March 25, 2007

3. "No permanent friends"
This chapter is based largely on "Portrait of a pragmatist: As a raw community organizer in Chicago in the '80s, Obama preached reaching out to attain goals," Bob Secter and John McCormick, Chicago Tribune, March 30, 2007
Material also taken from "Activism blossomed in college," Maurice Possley, Chicago Tribune, March 30, 2007

4. "Knock them all off"
This chapter is based largely on "Showing his bare knuckles: In first campaign, Obama revealed hard-edged, uncompromising side in eliminating party rivals," David Jackson and Ray Long, Chicago Tribune, April 4, 2007

5. "He had other ambitions"
This chapter is based largely on "Careful steps, looking ahead: After arriving in Springfield, Barack Obama proved cautious, but it was clear to many he had ambitions beyond the state Senate," Rick Pearson and Ray Long, Chicago Tribune, May 3, 2007

6. "Finding partners and coalitions"
This chapter is based largely on "Carefully crafting the Obama 'brand': From his first days in the U.S. Senate, the Illinoisan has followed a strategy envisioning a White House bid," Mike Dorning and Christi Parsons, Chicago Tribune, June 12, 2007
Material also taken from "Rezko owns vacant lot next to Obama's home," Ray Gibson and David Jackson, Chicago Tribune, Nov. 1, 2006
Material also used from a 2005 Chicago Tribune series on Obama's first year in the U.S. Senate by Jeff Zeleny

7. "Our souls are broken"
This chapter is based largely on "Barack's rock: Obama's blunt, tough partner Michelle helps shape her husband's politics and life and is integral to his campaign," Christi Parsons, Bruce Japsen and Bob Secter, Chicago Tribune, April 22, 2007

8. "Endless possibility"
An initial draft of this chapter was written by Mike Dorning
Some material taken from "Obama's formula: It's the network; Technology helped campaign take off — and change the game," by Christi Parsons and John McCormick, Chicago Tribune, May 25, 2008

9. "This is our moment"
An initial draft of this chapter was written by Mike Dorning, with additional material from John McCormick.

10. On the issues
barackobama.com; johnmccain.com; John McCormick; Chicago Tribune archives

PHOTOGRAPHS
Zbigniew Bzdak, Chicago Tribune: 6-7, 14, 86, 88-89, 104-105, 107, 108-109, 110-111, 112-113, 114 (top), 114 (bottom), 115, 118-119, front cover, back cover
Alex Garcia, Chicago Tribune: 126
Bruce Gilbert, Newsday: 117
Illinois state Senate: 44
Terrence Antonio James, Chicago Tribune: 40
John Lee, Chicago Tribune: 46, 49
Provided by Barack Obama: 22, 26, 27, 29, 33, 34-35, 42, 84
Charles Osgood, Chicago Tribune: 58-59
José M. Osorio, Chicago Tribune: 82, 103
Mike Mergen, for the Tribune: 90-91
Punahou yearbook: 31
Photo courtesy of Maya Soetoro-Ng: 20, 21, 25, 30, 39, 85
Pete Souza, Chicago Tribune: 8-9, 10-11, 60-61, 62-63, 65, 66-67, 68, 70-71, 73, 74-75, 76-77, 78-79, 80-81, 92-93, 94-95, 96-97, 98-99, 100-101
Nancy Stone, Chicago Tribune: 19
Scott Strazzante, Chicago Tribune: 51
Abel Uribe, Chicago Tribune: 54-55
E. Jason Wambsgans, Chicago Tribune: 52-53, 56-57

TYPEFACE
Hoefler Titling and Hoefler Text by Hoefler & Frere-Jones